Plains shield c. 1860-1880, 20'' d

PUBLISHER: Mary G. Hamilton

COVER: Shield cover, Cheyenne. Collected 1885. 55 cm diameter. Indian tanned buckskin, organic paints, red stroud cloth, eagle feathers. Attributed to Whirlwind. Dyer No. 614, Kansas City Museum No. 40.616. Photograph by Orville Crane. See article beginning on page 68.

EDITORIAL CONSULTANT: Norman Feder

STAFF: Pamela Forbes McLane, *Managing Editor*. Sharon W. Good, *Advertising Manager*. Carmen N. Nichols, *Editorial Assistant*.

SUBSCRIPTIONS: $12 yearly in the United States; $15 yearly in Canada and overseas by surface mail; $35 yearly overseas via air parcel post. Subscriptions should be mailed to the Circulation Department, *American Indian Art Magazine*, 7333 E. Monterey Way #5, Scottsdale, Arizona 85251. Wholesale inquiries welcome.

PUBLISHING OFFICE: 7333 E. Monterey Way #5, Scottsdale, Arizona 85251. (602) 994-5445. Application to mail at second class postage rates is pending at Scottsdale, Arizona.

Production and advertising design by Land O'Sun Printers, Inc. Color separations by Colorgraphics of Arizona. Printed by W. A. Krueger Company.

american indian art magazine

Autumn 1978
Volume 3, Number 4
August 1, 1978
SPECIAL PLAINS ISSUE

Fetish Figure. Bayaka, Zaire. Wood, lizard skin, cloth, tooth, shells. 28cm. Probably c. 1900. Cleveland Museum of Art, gift of Katherine C. White.

VINCE FOSTER

Fine early Plains collection

DEWEY-KOFRON GALLERY

112 east palace ave, santa fe, new mexico 87501   505-982-8478

affiliate: the kaibab shop/tucson

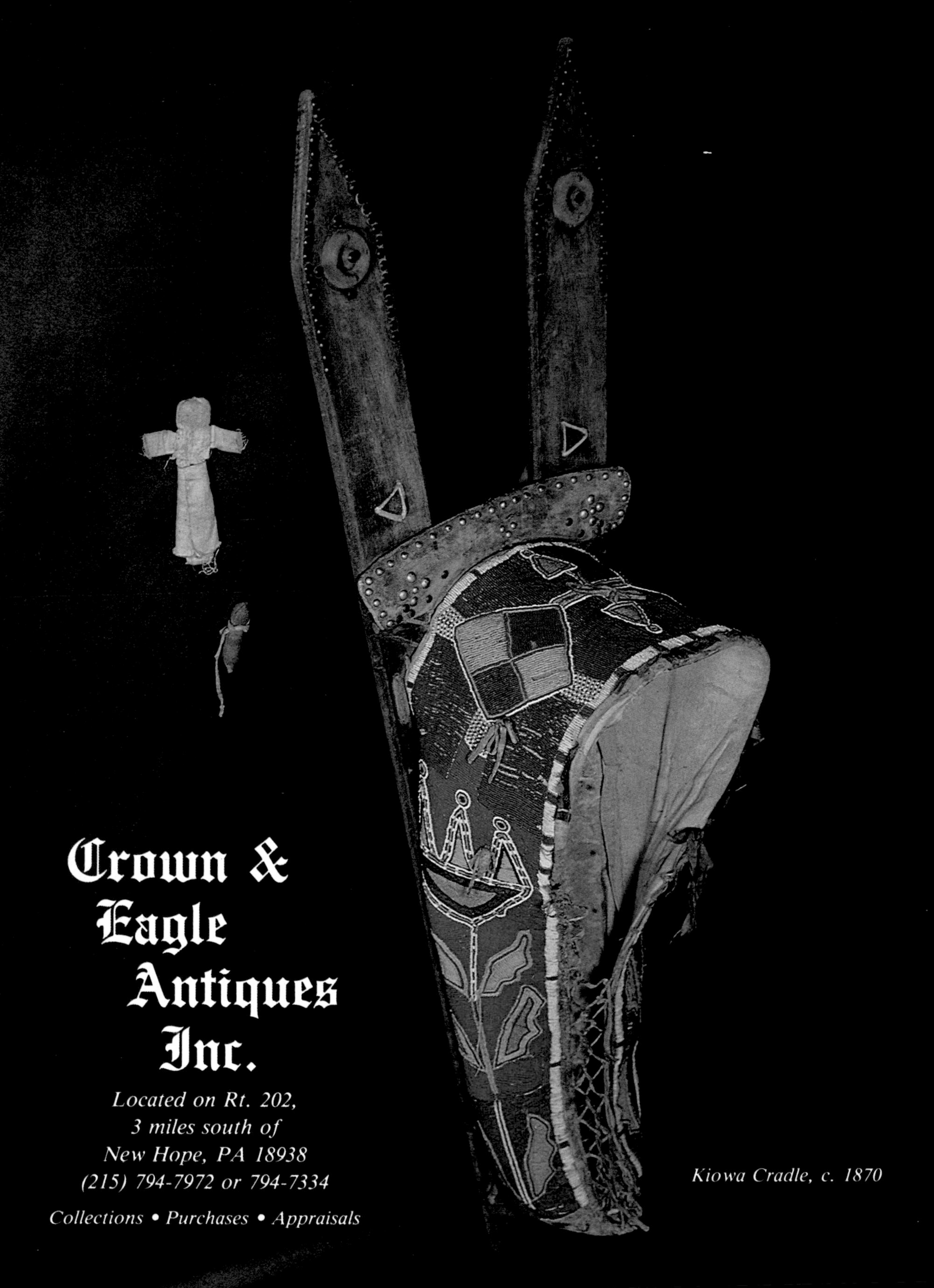

Kiowa Cradle, c. 1870

Specializing in museum quality art of the North American Indian,
Northwest Coast and Eskimo.

pendant by Mashongnaya

'Hopi gold-Hopi silver'

Kópavi International

P.O. Box 929 Garland Building Sedona, Arizona 86336 U.S.A. (602) 282-4774

Gallery open Wednesday-Sunday

RICHARD A. MEHAGIAN

LELOOSKA FAMILY GALLERY

5618 Lewis River Road • Ariel Washington 98603
By Appointment (206) 225-9522 • 225-9735

Featuring the work of
Lelooska
Shona-Hah
Patty Fawn
Yana
Tsungani
Na-Kwe-see
Kwunkwa-Dzi

NORTHWEST COAST ART
Woodcarving • Dolls • Jewelry

Dzoonokwa Mask by Lelooska
Chieftain Figure by Shona-Hah
Ivory Pendant by Patty Fawn

Gilbert Atencio

"Female Cloud Dancer" tempera 15" x 23"

One-Man Show
August 12-26

PREVIEW

August 11, 5:30 p.m.

GALLERIES

A.M. Indian Arts
Colorado Springs, Colorado
The Gallery is exhibiting the paintings of Helen Hardin, Jim Abeita, Robert Draper, and Irving Toddy. Also featured are lithographs by Fritz Scholder and R. C. Gorman.

Bayard Gallery
New York, New York
In October the Gallery will present "The Northwest Passage": Northwest Coast art of the nineteenth century and contemporary works by Lelooska, Pasco, Kidder, Davidson, Hamilton and Ksan artists.

The Bent-Box Gallery Ltd
Vancouver, British Columbia
The works of Nishga carver Norman Tait will be featured through August, including prints and works in wood, silver and gold. Posters for Robert Davidson's one-man exhibition (Nov. 21-Dec. 2) will be available in October for $12.50.

Gallery Three
Phoenix, Arizona
Exclusive representation of Gus Kniffin. The Gallery also shows the works of R. C. Gorman and Swazo.

The Indian Tree
Chicago, Illinois
The Gallery celebrates a move to larger space with an exhibit of prehistoric Southwestern pottery continuing through September. A showing of brass, silver and gold jewelry by Yazzie Johnson and Pueblo stoneware by Harold Littlebird will open on October 6 with a reception for the artists.

The Jamison Galleries
Santa Fe, New Mexico
A show for Earl Biss will be presented August 6-20; "Living Artists of the Santa Fe Area" will be exhibited October 6-21.

Linda McAdoo Gallery
Scottsdale, Arizona
In addition to the Scottsdale gallery, Linda McAdoo will be sharing the Gallery of the Southwest in Taos, New Mexico, with Jackson Hensely for the summer months. Earl Biss paintings and lithographs will be shown in both galleries.

The Squash Blossom
Colorado Springs, Colorado
Vail, Colorado
The Galleries feature contemporary Indian jewelry by Victor Beck, Jimmy King, Charles Loloma and Ben Nighthorse; pottery by Lonewolf, Goldenrod and Red Starr; paintings by Earl Biss, R C. Gorman and Kevin Red Star.

Galleries continued on page 18

Galleries continued from page 16

McGees Indian Den
Scottsdale, Arizona
The Gallery features revolving exhibits of Southwestern arts and crafts.

Old Santa Fe Trading Co.
Santa Fe, New Mexico
A show for San Ildefonso artist Gilbert Atencio will begin with a preview Friday, August 11, 6-9 p.m. The show will continue through August 26 with a reception on Friday, August 18.

Popovi Da Studio of Indian Arts
San Ildefonso Pueblo, New Mexico
Featured during August will be artists J. D. Roybal, Tony Da, Beatrin Yazz; potters Carlos and Carmelita Dunlap, Albert and Josephine Vigil, Helen Gutierrez, Pablita Chavarria, Elizabeth Naranjo, Mary Singer, Margaret and Luther Gutierrez. A permanent collection of pottery by Maria and Popovi and early potters from other pueblos is on display.

Potcarrier Indian Arts
Burlingame, California
Pottery by Goldenrod, Lois and Derek, and the Pueblo life paintings of John Garcia, all of Santa Clara Pueblo, will be featured in a special showing September 22-24 with the artists in attendance.

Snakebird Indian Arts
Little Rock, Arkansas
A one-man show of Mirac Creepingbear's work will be held August 14-25 in conjunction with the Ni-Wo-Di-Hi Gallery of Austin, Texas. A continuous showing of Plains Indian art will be exhibited at the Snakebird Gallery through December.

The Sun Dog
Austin, Texas
A special exhibit and sale of the works of potter Blue Corn and her daughter He'Shi Flower will be held October 20 with the artists in attendance. The work will remain in the Gallery indefinitely.

Tribal Customs Gallery
Houston, Texas
June 1 marked the opening of a new gallery in the Boarding House Village Shopping Center, Houston. Paintings of many new Plains Indian artists are on display,

West of the Moon Folk Art Gallery
San Francisco, California
"Decoration and Ritual in American Indian Art of the Plains" (Aug. 2-Sept. 16).

Winona Indian Trading Post
Santa Fe, New Mexico
A special display of Plains material including quilled and beaded shirts, pipes, tomahawks, beaded dresses and moccasins will continue through the summer.

PRIMITIVE ART, INC. Leonard Lasser 6 Orchard Rd. Windsor, Conn. 06095 203-688-4442

NORTH AMERICAN INDIAN ART GALLERY

AUCTION BLOCK

Harmer Johnson

Two very successful American Indian auctions took place — in New York City and in Scottsdale, Arizona — during the month of March. On March 3, Sotheby Parke Bernet, New York, held a pre-Columbian and American Indian sale; the North American section realized $94,225 for 146 sold lots. The highlight of the auction was a superb Aleut figurative lamp in the Kodiak tradition, Kachemak Stage, First Millennium. This piece sold for $26,000, the second highest price ever paid in an American public auction for an item of Indian or Eskimo art.[1]

In the same sale, a Northern Plains beaded and fringed hide shirt sold for $4,250, a Kiowa painted hide shirt and leggings that had belonged to the warrior Sitting Bear made $4,000, and a large Sioux Winter Count painted on muslin fetched $3,000. This Winter Count was of particular interest for it spanned the period from 1875 until 1952 and included the bombing of Pearl Harbor as well as the more traditional happenings.

Other prices of note included $2,000 paid for a Plains bearskin dance costume, $1,800 for an Assiniboin quilled pipe bag with catlinite and wooden pipe, $1,500 for a large Hopi kachina with elaborate tableta, $1,300 for a Sioux beaded hide cradle cover, and $1,100 for a Navajo concha belt.

The Scottsdale auction (March 17-19) of the Col. Doug Allard Collection realized $385,352.50 for 1,000 lots. This was the most important sale since the C. G. Wallace Collection went on the block in Phoenix in 1975, both in terms of the number of lots sold and the prices realized. The auction included material in all mediums and from all Indian cultures, whereas the Wallace sale contained almost nothing but jewelry. From this point of view it was extremely significant in terms of the current state of the American Indian art market, for the prices realized in all areas were very strong, showing a depth to the market which many collectors and dealers had seriously doubted.

The highest price — $7,000 — was paid for a Mission "circus basket," c.1885. This fine vessel was woven with seventeen figures of circus animals, possibly copied from an early circus poster or train.

Baskets fetched good prices throughout the sale: $4,500 (Chilkotin storage basket), $4,000 (Pan-

[1]The highest price was $36,000 paid at Sotheby Parke Bernet, New York, on November 14, 1973, for a Salish wooden spindle whorl (See *American Indian Art Magazine*, Summer 1975).

amint basket with deer, trees, bows and arrows), $3,500 (Maidu feast basket), $2,850 (Apache grain barrel), $2,700 (Attu cylindrical lidded basket), $2,100 (Tulare storage basket), $2,100 (Skokomish storage basket).

A pair of Lelooska carved totem poles, each eight feet high, sold for $5,250, and a Kwakiutl model totem pole carved by Charlie James c. 1905 made $2,900.

Other impressive prices included $4,500 for a rare nineteenth century Zuni cow kachina, $4,000 (Blackfeet painted and beaded hide shirt), $4,000 (Flathead beaded hide war shirt), $3,200 (Crow beaded buffalo hide martingale), $2,750 (Chilkat apron), $2,750 (Kiowa? beaded baby carrier), $2,100 (Zuni pottery kiva vessel molded with frogs), $2,000 (pair of Sioux quilled hide "possible bags"), and $2,000 (Germantown eye-dazzler blanket).

Another major sale of American Indian art was held at Christie's in London on June 13 which included the Megginch Indian relics, the property of The Lord Strange. The collection, assembled by General Sir Gordon Drummond (1772-1854), consisted of eastern Canadian and Northeastern Indian material. Highlights of the sale were two Naskapi painted caribou skin men's coats c.1770 and a superb eighteenth century Great Lakes quilled headdress, probably Potawatomi. Detailed results of this auction will appear in a subsequent issue of *American Indian Art Magazine*.

AMERICAN INDIAN ART MAGAZINE

7333 EAST MONTEREY WAY, SUITE 5, SCOTTSDALE, ARIZONA 85251

AMERICAN INDIAN ART MAGAZINE is published four times a year. It features articles on all the arts of American Indians—from jewelry, pottery, textiles, and baskets through painting and sculpture. Many handsome photographs accompany these articles. A perfect gift for anyone interested in the native culture of this hemisphere.

Subscription rates: $12.00/year U.S.; $24.00/two years U.S.; $15.00/year Canada and other foreign countries; $35.00/year for overseas Air Parcel Post (U.S. funds please). Please allow 6-8 weeks for your first issue.

Also available: binders to hold one year's subscription (4 copies) $13.50 each. Bound volumes—four issues in handsome hardbound books for permanent reference $26.50 each.
Volume 1 Nov. '75-Aug. '76
Volume 2 Nov. '76-Aug. '77
Volume 3 (available after Sept. '78) Nov. '77-Aug. '78

SUBSCRIBER'S NAME ______

ADDRESS ______

CITY ______

STATE ______ ZIP ______

☐ NEW SUBSCRIBER ☐ RENEWAL

GIFT FOR ______

ADDRESS ______

CITY ______

STATE ______ ZIP ______

BINDERS QTY______ $______

BOUND VOL 1 QTY______ $______

BOUND VOL 2 QTY______ $______

BOUND VOL 3 QTY______ $______

AMOUNT ENCLOSED $______

CHARGE TO VISA ACCT. # ______

EXPIRATION DATE: ______

MASTER CHARGE ACCT. # ______

EXPIRATION DATE: ______

______
Signature

RETURN ADDRESS

PLACE
STAMP
HERE

AMERICAN INDIAN ART MAGAZINE

7333 E. MONTEREY WAY,
Suite 5
SCOTTSDALE, AZ 85251

Attn: Circulation Manager

MUSEUMS

Alaska State Museum
Juneau, Alaska
"Wood — An Alaskan Art Form," an exhibit of wood artifacts by Alaskan woodworkers including works of early Eskimo, Tlingit and Haida carvers as well as contemporary works.

Anchorage Historical and Fine Arts Museum
Anchorage, Alaska
"Survival: Life and Art of the Alaskan Eskimo" will be exhibited through August 13.

Arizona State Museum
Tucson, Arizona
"Sacred Paths — Aspects of the Native American and Hispanic Religious Experience in the Southwest," (Sept. 1-Nov. 30).

British Columbia Provincial Museum
Victoria, British Columbia
"Quills, Beads and Threads: Athapascan Decorative Art," an exhibit of British Columbian Athapaskan quillwork, beadwork and silk thread embroidery (through December 31.)

Buffalo Bill Historical Center
Cody, Wyoming
"Michael Coleman Paintings" an exhibit of 49 recent works — many of Plains Indians — will be on view through September 30. A catalogue is available for $5.70 including postage. Permanent features at the Center include the Buffalo Bill Museum, Whitney Gallery of Western Art, Plains Indian Museum, and Winchester Museum.

Colorado Springs Fine Arts Center
Colorado Springs, Colorado
"Southwest Indian Arts: A Study of Styles," an exhibition showing the variety of styles and techniques in baskets, ceramics and textiles of the major Southwest tribes will continue through September 10.

Denver Museum of Natural History
Denver, Colorado
The Mary W. A. and Francis V. Crane American Indian Hall opened in its entirety May 19 (see *American Indian Art Magazine*, Summer 1978). The Hall honors the achievements of Indians from seven culture areas ranging from Arctic Alaska to the Florida Everglades.

Frederick S. Wight Art Gallery
University of California, Los Angeles
"Moche Art of Peru: Pre-Columbian Symbolic Communication" (Oct. 10-Nov. 26) is the first major exhibition devoted exclusively to the art and culture of the Moche civilization in Northern Peru. An illustrated catalogue will be available.

Museums continued on page 26

Museums continued from page 25

Haffenreffer Museum of Anthropology — Brown University
Bristol, Rhode Island

"California Indians in Paint and Brush" runs through August 31. An exhibit of prehistoric and historic coastal Algonkian material will coincide with publication of a new catalogue of Wampanoag artifacts from Rhode Island. In the fall, a special Plains exhibit will be accompanied by a catalogue of the Plains material in the Museum's collection.

The Heard Museum
Phoenix, Arizona

"The Martinez Tradition," featuring the pottery of Maria Martinez and her relatives will continue through August.

Hopi Cultural Center Museum
Second Mesa, Arizona

The Artist Hopid will hold their fifth annual exhibition through September 3.

Indian Pueblo Cultural Center
Albuquerque, New Mexico

The Center's anniversary celebration will feature a feast, Pueblo dancers and other festivities (August 26-27). Paintings by Charles Lovato and jewelry by Raymond Tafoya (through August 24); pueblo paintings (Aug. 20-Oct. 9); Patrick Swazo Hinds Memorial Show (Oct. 15-Dec. 15).

Kansas City Museum of History and Science
Kansas City, Missouri

The Dyer Collection of Plains Indian material (see pp. 68-73) can be viewed in "open storage" with the rest of the Museum's North American Indian collection. The catalogue of the photographic exhibition "Crying for a Vision," a saga of reservation life at Rosebud, South Dakota, is available for $8.00 including postage.

Maxwell Museum of Anthropology
Albuquerque, New Mexico

Jewelry of the Prehistoric Southwest by E. Wesley Jernigan, is the basis of an exhibition of Hohokam, Mogollon, and Anasazi jewelry (through September 17). Jernigan's book, published under the auspices of the School for American Research, is available through the giftshop for $24.95.

Millicent Rogers Museum
Taos, New Mexico

The newly opened museum store carries prehistoric, historic and contemporary American Indian and Spanish Colonial artifacts as well as books on Southwestern subjects.

Minneapolis Institute of Arts
Minneapolis, Minnesota

"I Wear the Morning Star," the exhibit of American Indian Ghost Dance clothing, music, and photo-

Museums continued on page 30

VINTAGE, ORIGINAL
PHOTOGRAPHS OF INDIANS
& THE WEST BY WITTICK,
VROMAN, HILLERS, CURTIS
& OTHERS . . .
FINE INDIAN ART,
ANTIQUITIES,
OLD PRINTS AND MAPS

PACKARDS
INDIAN TRADING COMPANY
Santa Fe
New Mexico
Charter Member Indian Arts & Crafts Association
Navajo Silver Smith

Catalogue Review

ARTIFICIAL CURIOSITIES: An exposition of Native Manufactures, collected on the Three Pacific Voyages of Captain James Cook, R.N. by Adrienne L. Kaeppler. (Special Publication 65, Honolulu, Hawaii: Bishop Museum Press, 1978. xvi + 294 pp., illustrations, color plates, $27.50.) Reviewed by Norman Feder.

This is the catalogue to accompany the major exhibit at the Bernice Pauahi Bishop Museum in Honolulu (January 18-August 31); "on the occasion of the bicentennial of the European discovery of the Hawaiian Islands by Captain Cook January 18, 1778."

The specimens collected by the sailors and officers of Cook's third voyage were widely scattered after their return to England, but the bulk of the material evidently went to Sir Ashton Lever for display in his private museum. The Leverian Museum was sold by public lottery in 1786 and later resold by public auction in 1806. The auction, consisting of 7,800 lots, lasted 65 days and further dispersed the collection. For the past eight years, Adrienne L. Kaeppler has been trying to locate all of the documented Cook pieces in museums and private collections. This is not an easy task because there is a general lack of documentation on all early collections. Furthermore, there are questionable attributions to Cook on many artifacts on the basis of their early style or due to wishful thinking on the part of curators or collectors.

Kaeppler claims to have traced more than 2,000 documented pieces from Cook's three voyages and to have assembled more than 400 of these for the Bishop Museum exhibit. The catalogue lists all of the ethnographic pieces which Kaeppler accepts as documented Cook objects; however, many are documented by "strong circumstantial evidence" only. The 622 illustrations include photographs of most of the 400 items borrowed for the exhibit, plus many photographs of items not borrowed, so that the catalogue will serve as a valuable reference tool for future research.

Clearly Kaeppler has accomplished more than any previous scholar in tracing the early dispersal of Cook voyage artifacts and in tracking down their present locations. While it is evident that a vast quantity of Cook voyage artifacts in museum collections can never be positively attributed to Cook because of lost documentation, the reader is left with the uneasy feeling that Kaeppler knows a lot more than she is willing to tell in this volume. She tantalizes us with comments such as:

> "The information on all Cook voyage objects known, as far as I have been able to sort it out, is included here. Not all detail or conclusions on significance are included and the reader is referred to my past and forthcoming studies" (p. 48).

> "The information for all objects noted, 'Leverian Museum' will be included in my forthcoming volume, *Captain James Cook, Sir Ashton Lever,* and *Miss Sarah Stone* to be published by Bishop Museum Press" (p. 49).

A large number of the pieces attributed to Cook in the British Museum (and a few in other museums) are not included in Kaeppler's inventory because of questionable documentation. While Kaeppler's concern for adequate and reliable documentation is certainly understandable, I cannot help wishing that these pieces were also included, perhaps as a separate section on items of questionable documentation.

Readers of *American Indian Art Magazine* will be interested in knowing that the major portion of this catalogue covers collections from the various Pacific Islands visited by Cook on his three voyages. Only 23 pages of the text are devoted to North America (pp. 251-271 and 274-277), but this includes 59 illustrations. Twenty-nine objects from North America were actually borrowed for the exhibit.

Hopefully the Cook bicentennial has renewed the interest in early artifacts, and we can look forward to future publications by Kaeppler and others which will give us a clearer picture of aboriginal material culture before European contact.

Captain James Cook arrived at Nootka Sound on the west coast of Vancouver Island on March 29, 1778, and thereby established the English claim to what is now British Columbia. The Cook bicentennial is also being celebrated in Canada, where a small but important exhibit of Cook artifacts has been organized by Lynn Maranda at the Vancouver, British Columbia, Centennial Museum. This exhibition, "Discovery 1778: Captain James Cook and the Peoples of the Pacific," runs through September 6; it includes material from the Pacific Islands as well as 58 items from the Northwest Coast. A short illustrated catalogue-checklist is available from the Museum for $1.34 including mailing.

Museums continued from page 26

graphs is completing its long tour with stops at the National Museum of Man, Ottawa, Canada, June-August and at The Tweed Gallery of the University of Minnesota / Duluth, September-November. The catalogue and a 28-minute color videotape of the exhibit are available.

Museum of Northern Arizona
Flagstaff, Arizona
The Museum's 50th Anniversary Show (October 1-29) will utilize the entire museum area for display of the most significant pieces from the collections, in addition to old photographs and other representations of the Museum's history.

Museum of the American Indian, Heye Foundation
New York, New York
"Echoes of the Drums" will be showing Aug. 15-Oct. 31 at the U.S. Customs House, Bowling Green, New York City.

Museum of the Plains Indian and Crafts Center
Browning, Montana
"Contemporary Plains Indian Arts and Crafts" (through September 30). "Two Feathers," interiors — stained glass by Betty Lee and Fae Shelby, Blackfeet (Sept. 17-Nov. 3). Also on view is "Winds of Change," a multimedia presentation about the evolution of Indian cultures on the Northern Plains.

Red Rock State Park
Gallup, New Mexico
The Intertribal Indian Ceremonial will be held August 10-13.

Saint Joseph Museum
St. Joseph, Missouri
The Museum's permanent exhibits show Indian arts, crafts, and lifestyles circa 1890.

San Diego Museum of Man
San Diego, California
"Man the Hunter," a new permanent exhibit of the geographical environment and weapons used by the Eskimo, Northwest Coast and Plains Indians, opens this summer. A "Tribal Arts Fair" (August 25-27) will feature crafts demonstrations; many items, old and new, will be for sale.

Sioux Indian Museum and Crafts Center
Rapid City, South Dakota
"Contemporary Sioux Indian Arts and Crafts" (through Sept. 30); photographs by Charles and Carlin Red Blanket, Oglala Sioux (Oct. 1-Nov. 3).

Smithsonian Institution – Renwick Gallery
Washington, D.C.
"Maria Martinez: Five Generations of Potters" continues through August. An illustrated catalogue by Susan Peterson, author of *The Living Tradition of Maria Martinez,* will be available.

Museums continued on page 76

First Class
Permit No. 3303
Austin, Texas

BUSINESS REPLY MAIL
no postage necessary if mailed in the United States

NI-WO-DI-HI GALLERIES

9th & Rio Grande
Post Office Box 746
Austin, Texas 78767

First Class
Permit No. 3303
Austn, Texas

BUSINESS REPLY MAIL
no postage necessary if mailed in the United States

NI-WO-DI-HI GALLERIES

9th & Rio Grande
Post Office Box 746
Austin, Texas 78767

signed

ART

The m... ct a unique way of life
and a... pecializes in the finest
painti... ghout the country. Include... Roye, Virginia Stroud,
Johnn... n here are a pair of the
limite... literature on all works
curre...

Bill McLemore

1

The Masked Dandy

William Benton

An Indian sits in a beautiful white wicker chair. He wears a fur hat with a single feather in it, cocked at an angle. Legs crossed. His stare is defiant, stern. A hint of posed gruffness. He is dressed fit to kill. A paisley scarf dwarfed by a necklace of bear claws and feathers. A bright purple shirt with orange polka dots, aquamarine vest, blue and white trousers with red stripes. Red and white moccasins: pink socks. He sits in an interior. There is a Navajo rug beneath the wicker chair. On the wall behind him hangs a reproduction of Van Gogh's "Wheatfield." The wall seems to be a construction of tarpaper and two-by-fours studded with shiny metal hearts. Perhaps it is wallpaper. There are two windows which look out on dry hills and small clouds. A border of gold containing red and green mica-flake shapes frames the edge of the picture. The painting is called "Collector #5" (Fig. 1).

Printed as a poster for the T. C. Cannon exhibition in 1976 at the Museum of Navajo Ceremonial Art in Santa Fe, this painting has since become one of the hallmark images of contemporary Indian art.

The painting is almost an apotheosis of what Cannon does. Underpainting seen through thin glazes of color is a formal concern present in most of Cannon's work. It is a lyrical excellence which he ties to objects in a way that stresses their emotional order. The prettiness of such painting doesn't seem sentimental, but rather *gentle,* as it handles objects whose actuality in the world elicits homage. A time more pertinent than our own to the life of the Navajo rug maker becomes a fragile fact in the way a rug is painted. However, in Cannon's work, these are elements, sensitively articulating what is finally a contemporary impulse: a direct vocabulary of decoration.

More: a logic operates in Cannon's pictures that fits their decorativeness into patterns of meaning. In "Collector #5," there are almost antic signs of a sensibility manipulating aesthetic counters. The figure does not, in fact, sit with his legs crossed; he is in the *process* of crossing or uncrossing them. Either way, given the unfriendly expression on his face, it is unsettling. And either way, we feel a precise sense of what each would constitute in a little scenario, as we keep our eyes on him.

Cannon is not unaware of his mischief (he would be the first to hear the pun). His knowledge of the drama of gestures painted in mid-motion derives from Egon Scheile, whom he admires, which is itself mischievously erudite. Other painters important to him are Balthus, R. B. Kitaj, David Park, Richard Diebenkorn and Hunterwasser. A list almost suspiciously too pat. Unless . . .

Posit it. Cannon seems the elect of an aesthetic whose prototype in America is the dandy. He has, even, a painting entitled "Turn of the Century Dandy" (Fig. 2). The term is wistful, affectionate, ironic; and it permits, finally, a benignly amused intelligence to make

2

not only sense, but an aesthetic out of a world composed of Indian traditions, European *Kulture,* and an apocalyptic America.

Cannon sees the ornate, brightly arrayed Indian phenomenologically as a dandy. The subtler implication that a less colorful world imposed itself to create the contrast is scarcely formulated. It evaporates in the distances of pink skies. Cannon's paintings are of an earlier people, they exist in huge isolated spaces, where the relevance of their activities, rituals and regalia remains intact. They are, simply, beautiful. And if at some point the terms of that beauty are destined to lend themselves to the terms of satire, these are people never to know it. Their primitive decoration becomes the stuff of Cannon-the-dandy's decorative painting, which in turn creates and maintains the integrity of their lives. It is a decorous move by a thirty-one-year-old Kiowa painter, and fills with emotions deeper than those of the satirical logic that implements it.

"Catcher" (Fig. 3), "Grandmother in 1885" (Fig. 4), and "Cloud Madonna" (Fig. 5) are wonderful examples. In "Cloud Madonna," an Indian woman carries a black and white waterpot on her head as she walks toward a pueblo. The white areas of the pot are cloud-like, outlined in black against a purple sky. Behind her in the distance, a cloud cameos her profile, and one perceives the syzygy that is cloud at one end and painter's eye at the other — her face in the center. It is a picture which alludes to and eclipses the sophistication which has made it.

T. C. Cannon was born in Oklahoma in 1946. He studied at the Institute of American Indian Arts in Santa Fe, the San Francisco Art Institute, the College of Santa Fe, and Central State University in Edmond, Oklahoma. His list of exhibitions (over twenty of them) includes one-man shows at the Southern Plains Indian Museum, Anadarko, Oklahoma (1970), Pickard Galleries, Oklahoma City (1974), and The Wheelwright Museum, Santa Fe (1976); group shows in such places as Berlin, Turkey, Scot-

Bruce C. Jones

3

Bruce C. Jones

4

Bruce C. Jones

5

land; a two-man show with painter Fritz Scholder at the Smithsonian Institution in 1972. He was artist-in-residence at Colorado State University (1974), and at Dartmouth College (1975). Commissions include a mural for the Seattle Arts Commission, and for the Santa Fe Opera, a lithograph for the 1977 season and a poster for 1978.

At the Smithsonian exhibition, Cannon met New York dealer Jean Aberbach and his wife Susan. They purchased several paintings from the show, and by the fall of that year had begun to represent him on an exclusive basis. It has proved to be a lasting partnership. Cannon's first one-man show at the Aberbach Gallery is scheduled for October 1978.

Six years. Slowness is beauty, wrote the eminent economist Major Douglas. He had in mind, among other things that it was economically unsound that a painter be paid "by the piece" for his work, on the basis of supply and demand. He argued instead that payment be made to the artist as a *nurturing impulse*.

In his studio, Cannon interrupts, runs to a wall and removes a magazine clipping of a Balthus painting. "Six years!" he says. "He worked six years on it."

In "Self-Portrait in Studio," (Fig. 6) Cannon sits in a kitchen chair in front of a window that looks out onto a scene of Hunterwasser-like mountains. A drawing reminiscent of Matisse hangs on the wall, and below it, exactly on the same level with Cannon's head, a Dogon mask framed in red. Cannon, the masked dandy, wears a flowered shirt, sunglasses and a cream-colored stetson. He holds a cluster of paintbrushes in one hand. There are six of them.

William Benton owns the Clarke-Benton Gallery in Santa Fe.

On May 8, 1978, T. C. Cannon was killed in an automobile accident in Santa Fe. This article was finished several weeks before his death. T. C. had read the manuscript and was, he said, pleased with it. It therefore appears here as it was originally written. *Vale.* W.B.

Bruce C. Jones

1

PAWNEE CRADLEBOARDS

Norman Feder

Introduction

Most of the design elements used by Plains Indians seem to have no symbolic significance. There are, of course, some exceptions such as the designs painted on bison robes, old war shirts, and leggings; but although we can be fairly certain that these painted designs do have symbolic meaning, the meaning of most of the symbols has long been forgotten and has not been adequately recorded.

Among most Indian groups "birth" was considered a special blessing and somewhat of a mystery. Infant mortality rates were quite high. As a result, a tremendous amount of ceremony was developed around birth and at least the first year of infant care. This seems to be particularly true for the Pawnee and their Caddoan relatives.

This article will attempt to show that the Pawnee developed a tribally distinctive cradleboard type; that the designs on Pawnee cradleboards do have symbolic meaning; and that elaborate ritual and ceremony developed around birth and infant care. Finally it will briefly discuss cradleboards and infant care among related tribes.

The Pawnee Cradleboard

The Pawnee cradleboard is of the general Prairie Siouan type: a single flat board with an attached hoop, but without the central Algonquian movable footboard. Traditionally Pawnee cradleboards are slightly wider at the bottom. About seven to eight inches from the bottom, the board is cut in to form a step on each edge. This step serves to prevent the straps which secure the baby in place from slipping down and off the bottom of the board (a feature which is also found on old Omaha boards, and probably Ponca as well). Another characteristic of Pawnee cradleboards is that the tie thong which holds the hoop in place originates from the center of the top design panel. However, the main feature which distinguishes Pawnee cradleboards from those of other Prairie tribes is the nature of the design carved and painted on the upper third of the board.

Origin Legends and Design Symbolism

Pawnee star lore is well-known (Fletcher 1902, 1903). The Pawnee explain the origin of their distinctive cradle designs in an ancient myth relating to the Morning Star ceremony. Several versions of this myth are recorded in the literature. Curtis states:

Among the Pawnees the husband brings to his wife the cradle-board. This is ceremonially cut from a tree by the husband's kinsman, and decorated with

1. *Cradleboard, Pawnee, c.1820? Carved, painted cottonwood plank. 92.8 cm high, 35 cm wide (top), 29.8 cm wide (bottom). British Museum 5196. Presented by A. W. Franks, January 1, 1869; purchased by Franks from Umlauf, a Hamburg dealer, December 11, 1868. According to J. C. H. King of the British Museum, this was conceivably part of a collection formed by Paul Wilhelm, Duke of Württemberg, as other items purchased by Franks from Umlauf at the same time are credited to Duke Paul. Duke Paul visited the Pawnee on his first trip to the United States 1822-1824. The cradleboard may date from this trip, although Duke Paul continued to make visits to the United States as late as 1857. Duke Paul died in 1860; his collection was dispersed mostly to museums in Stuttgart and Berlin. Photograph courtesy the British Museum.*

symbolic emblems. . . . There is a detailed legend of how the Morning Star won the cradle-board, which hung with many other cradle-boards upon posts within a lodge in the heavens. These cradle-boards were decorated with emblematic designs, which the people of earth now use to decorate their cradle-boards. Thus the Pawnee say that their designs came from the stars (Curtis 1907: 101-102 footnotes).

A slightly different version of this story is recorded by Frances Densmore, and will be quoted here because of the reference to the symbolic meanings:

Finally she [Evening Star] insisted that he [Morning Star] make provisions for the child that should be born; she even required him to provide perfumed water for bathing the child and a cradle board in which it should be placed. On the hoop, or arch, of this cradle board was painted a morning star and the lightnings, this custom being followed by the Pawnee at the present time (Densmore 1929: 21).

There are several other references to symbolism on Pawnee cradles. Dorsey mentions a cradle whose head part had a painting of the sun (Dorsey 1904a: 204). Fletcher states:

The spots of the wildcat skin used for a cover symbolized the stars, the bow the sky, and the crooked furrow cut thereon signified the lightning, whose power was typified by the arrows tied to the bow. All the parts were symbolic (Quoted in Mason 1910: 358).

Natalie Curtis says:

The board should be of cottonwood; the covering, a speckled wild-cat-skin, emblem of the starry heavens. With strips of otter-skin should the child be bound upon the board; for the otter lives in the water, and betokens the rain-storms.

Above the board, over the head of the child, should be stretched a hoop, cut from the willow-tree. This too betokens the rain-storm, also the Arch-Above-the-Earth — the Rainbow (Curtis 1907: 101-102).

Natalie Curtis also shows a drawing of a Pawnee cradleboard painted by a Pawnee woman. The drawing is captioned: "Cradle-board for the Morning Star Clan" and reads:

Upon this cradle-board have been bound the children of Sakuruta [the Indian name of Coming Sun or James R. Murie] and his wife. Above the head of the child, at the top of the board, are painted the morning star, flint arrow-heads, and the rainbow. The design tells that the child is under the protection of the morning star and is watched over by the Powers of the West, because of the rainbow (Curtis 1907: 103).

The American Museum of Natural History has a small sized cradle (Cat. No. 50.1/8411) collected by James R. Murie in 1915. This is very similar to the cradle illustrated in Curtis and may represent the same design (Fig. 6).

To sum up the somewhat conflicting data on cradle symbolism, we find that there are frequent references to stars and particularly the Morning Star, the Sun, lightning, rainbows, arrows or arrowheads, the sky, and rain or water. An examination of Pawnee cradleboard designs on collected examples and in field photographs seem to show that the common

Text continues on page 45

2,2a. *Cradleboard, Pawnee, c.1806? Carved, painted cottonwood plank. 29¾"h x 11½"w. Nebraska State Historical Society A-264. Recovered archeologically from the Hill Site (25 WT 1) grave No. 32 of a small child. The site is located between the towns of Red Cloud and Guide Rock in Webster County, Nebraska, on the south side of the Republican River. This Republican band village is believed to have been the village visited by Pike in 1806. It was abandoned by 1815. Photograph courtesy Nebraska State Historical Society,* **2a.** *Reconstruction of the design.*

3,3a. *Cradleboard, Pawnee, c.1830? Carved, painted cottonwood plank. 35"h x 11"w. Nebraska State Historical Society 25 PK 1-390/1. Recovered archeologically from an infant burial No. 21 of Burial Hill 4 on the Clarks Site (25 PK 1). The site is located three miles southeast of the town of Clarks in Polk County, Nebraska, on the south side of the Platte River. The site was identified by Wedel as a Grand Pawnee village of the 1820-1845 period. The photograph shows the cradleboard before it was removed from the ground. This is the only Pawnee cradleboard found by the author which has the design panel divided into four parts. Photograph courtesy Nebraska State Historical Society.* **3a.** *Reconstruction of the design.*

4. *Cradleboard, Pawnee, c.1900? Carved, painted cottonwood plank. Size unknown as it is currently on display and could not be measured. FMNH 59381. Collected by George A. Dorsey in 1901 in Pawnee County, Oklahoma. The center panel design is unique, but the border is a standard type. Photograph courtesy Field Museum of Natural History.*

5. *Cradleboard, Pawnee, c.1900? Carved, painted cottonwood plank. There is no data available on this example. It was at one time on display in a museum in Ponca City, Oklahoma, but its present location is unknown. The design is a very typical four-pointed star with lightning border. Photograph by Ben Stone.*

6. *Cradleboard, Pawnee, c.1900? Carved, painted cottonwood plank. Small size, either a model or for a newborn infant. AMNH 50.1/8411. Collected by James R. Murie in 1915 in Oklahoma. This is very similar to a cradleboard sketched in Curtis 1907, p. 103, listed as being used by the children of James R. Murie. Photograph courtesy American Museum of Natural History.*

2

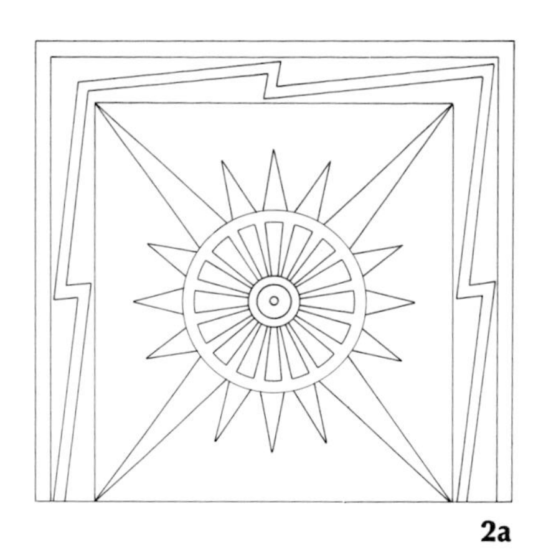

2a

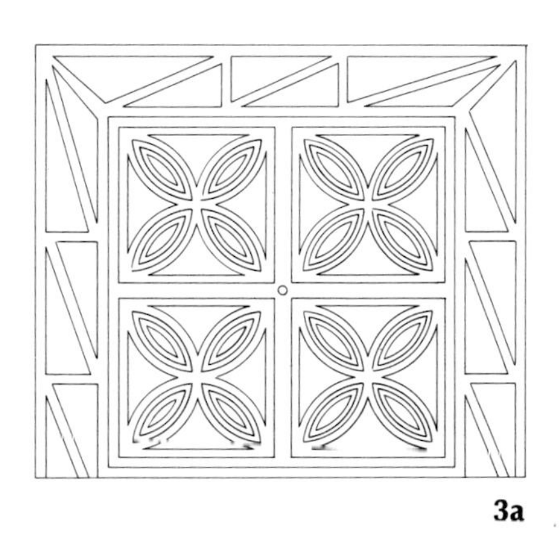

3a

3

4

5

6

7

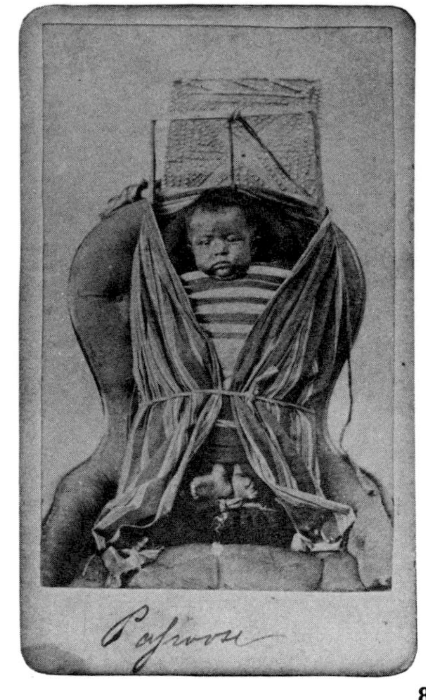

8

7. *A Pawnee family with cradleboard. The design is a standard morning star, very similar to* **5.** *Photograph by Prettyman in the Cunningham Collection. Photograph courtesy of the Western History Collection, University of Oklahoma Library.*

8. *Pawnee? infant in cradleboard. Same center panel design as* **5,7.** *On this example, the design appears to be outlined with brass tacks but not carved into the wood. From a carte de visite photograph by Eaton's Gallery of Art in Omaha, Nebraska, c.1860s. Copy print from an original in the Chandler-Pohrt Collection.*

9,9a. *Interior of a Pawnee earth lodge showing Pawnee and Wichita cradleboards. Detail of an old photograph by Melvin R. Gilmore of Bethany, Nebraska (date not recorded). Photograph courtesy Nebraska State Historical Society.* **9a.** *Reconstruction of the Pawnee design, which seems to be a variation of* **6.**

9

9a

central design is a four-pointed star, but that this is often combined with a multirayed sun symbol. The elaborate borders seem to fall into three basic styles which probably represent either lightning or rainbows.

It may be that there are traditionally a set number of basic designs all originally acquired by Morning Star from the lodge in the heavens as told in the origin legend, but if this is so, the basic designs have undergone some variations with time. It may also be possible that some specific designs were used by only certain families, or by certain clans, or even by different political bands. The evidence on hand is not sufficient to answer these questions.

Miscellaneous Notes on Pawnee Cradleboards

Most authors agree that Pawnee cradleboards were made from cottonwood, but Dorsey also mentions the use of elm:

> In olden times, at the first signs of pregnancy of the wife, the grandmothers notified the wife's relatives to prepare an elm baby-board and the husband's relatives a board of cottonwood (Dorsey and Murie 1940: 91).

It is also possible that the board was cut from a living tree. According to Fletcher:

> The tree for the Pawnee cradle-board was carefully selected, and the middle taken out so that the heart of life should be preserved, else the child would die. Equal care was taken that the head of the cradle should follow the grain (Mason 1910: 358).

While the above does not specifically state that a living tree was used, it does imply as much; and we have specific information for other tribes. Skinner mentions for the Sauk:

> Cradle boards of the general central Algonkian type, with movable foot boards, were used to carry children. They were made from the wood of living trees, just as are the false-faces of the Iroquois. The idea seems to be that of a sympathetic connection between the life of the tree and that of the child. Cradle boards made of cut or seasoned wood, or of white-man's boards, are deemed unlucky (Skinner 1925: 137).

Finally it might be of interest to note that Pawnee cradleboards seem to have changed little from the earliest known example (Fig. 2) dating from about 1806 to those collected in the early years of the twentieth century (Fig. 6). However, present-day Pawnee seem to have forgotten their older traditions. Dr. James Howard has supplied the author with a sketch of a cradleboard made by George Little Sun in 1976, but it looks more like a typical Osage design than a Pawnee one.

Pawnee Relationships and Affiliations

The Pawnee tribe is actually composed of four politically independent groups known as bands who lived apart from each other on the Republican and Platte Rivers and their tributaries in Nebraska and Kansas. These four bands are: Skidi (also known as Pawnee Loups or Wolf Band); Kitkehaxki (also known as Republican or Little Earth Lodge Band); Tsawi (also known as Grand or Asking for Meat Band); and the Pitahawirata (also known as Tapage or Man Going Down Stream Band). These four groups were placed on a joint reservation in Nebraska, but were moved to their present Oklahoma location in 1874.

The Pawnee were usually at war with the Dakota, Kiowa, Comanche, Cheyenne, Arapaho, Osage, and Kaw; but were on friendly terms with the Omaha, Ponca and Oto. They kept up friendly trade relations with the Arikara, Mandan, and Wichita.

Linguistically the Pawnee speak a Caddoan language in common with the Wichita (also known as Pawnee Picts), the Arikara, Caddo, Kichai, Waco, Tawakoni, and Taovaya. The Skidi Pawnee are somewhat closer linguistically to the Arikara than to other Pawnee. In addition some Skidi moved far to the southwest and joined the Wichita about 1770 (Hughes 1974).

It is important to understand the relationships outlined above in order to trace diffusion and borrowing patterns. For example, the Omaha and Ponca have cradleboards that are somewhat similar to those of the Pawnee in having the stepped notch near the bottom and even in the use of some star designs (Figs. 10 and 11). The Wichita-Pawnee relationship accounts for the fact that both typical Wichita and Pawnee cradles are shown side by side in the photo of the interior of a Pawnee earth lodge (Fig. 9). And, as we will see below, the mythology pertaining to Wichita cradles is somewhat similar to that of the Pawnee.

The Wichita Cradle

The Wichita are of Caddoan stock and they maintained friendly trade relations with the Pawnee, visited each other frequently and even intermarried. Dorsey sums up Wichita religious beliefs by stating:

> The religion of the Wichita, like that of the Pawnee, though to a less extent, may be characterized as a star cult (Dorsey 1904b: 18).

Dorsey also presents a rather complete account of the Wichita cradle:

Shortly after the birth of the child the father looked about the village to discover some woman who had grown fast and who had always had good health. His choice having been made he went to the timber and cut twenty-four small, slender willow rods, the longest of which, to form the sides of the cradle, were cut first. Before the stick was cut he addressed it: "Now you were made to be used for many different purposes. I have now come to take your life. You are to be used for a cradle." Standing on the south, he cut the stick on the east side, then stepping to the west of the stick, he cut it on the south side. He then stepped to the north and cut it on the west side, and then he took hold of the stick and made it fall towards the north. He then trimmed the sticks and cut them into the proper length. During this time he neither sang nor made any noise. Having cut the twenty-four sticks, he returned home. He now decorticated the rods, carefully saving the bark. He dried and straightened the rods, and if any were too large he trimmed them down. The shavings also were carefully saved. The rods having been prepared he took them, together with the bark and shavings, to the woman he had selected. She took the bark and the shavings toward the north and hid them either in a tree or in the ground; otherwise the growth and health of the child would have been impaired. Returning to her lodge she took up the twenty-four rods, prayed to the Man-never-known-on-Earth, then to the Moon, that as she made the cradle they would help her to make it in a proper manner, and that the child might grow rapidly. The sticks were then painted red or yellow and were bound together in the form of a flat mat by sinew from the back of the neck of a buffalo. As soon as the cradle was finished she took it to the parents, and handed it to the mother, telling her that she had finished the cradle; that while making it she had prayed to the maker of all things and to the moon; and that the moon would see to it that the child would grow rapidly and be healthy. As soon as the child began to walk the cradle was put aside and kept for future use in the same family. A cradle which had served for several children in one family, all of whom had been healthy might be sought after by another family, believing that by the use of it their children would grow without sickness or any trouble. Should the child die during its cradle days the cradle was carried out and placed upon a tree, that it might never be used again (Dorsey 1904b: 11-12).

A very similar account is recorded by Edward Curtis, who adds that the

Bark and shavings were carefully hidden lest they fall into the hands of witches (Curtis 1930: 40-41).

Mason calls this type of baby carrier a "Hurdle Cradle" (Figs. 12 and 13) and describes it as follows:

These consist of a number of rods or small canes or sticks arranged in a plane on an oblong hoop and held in place by lashing with splints or cords. The Yuman tribes and the Wichita so made them (Mason 1907-1910: 358).

In all probability the Hurdle Cradle was the ancient Caddoan type, since the type is recorded archaeologically for the Southeast. Dellinger describes some prehistoric cradles found in caves from the Ozark Bluff Dwellers of Arkansas as an "Oval frame set longitudinally with reeds united by open twining (Dellinger 1936). The true cradleboard (a single flat board) was most likely a central Algonquian style which diffused to the Prairie Siouans and lost the movable footboard in the process. The Pawnee probably adopted the flat board style from the Prairie Siouans (Omaha and Ponca). Some Prairie Siouans, like the Iowa, continued to make both the central Algonquian and the Prairie type cradleboards into recent times (Skinner 1926: 280-281).

Dorsey records an interesting Wichita tradition regarding the disposal of the placenta:

The after-birth was always wrapped in cloth and placed in a straight young elm tree — the elm tree because it produced splendid, straight offspring which grew well, and always seem prosperous. They prayed to the tree: "keep this until it decays. I beg that the child which was in this may have power. May it grow like your children." The after-birth was

Text continues on page 48

10. *Cradleboard, Omaha, c.1880? Cottonwood plank, 38½"h. MAI 20/1373. Collected by the artist, De Cost Smith, probably on the Omaha Reservation at Macy, Nebraska. Unlike the Pawnee examples this is not carved, just painted and outlined with brass tacks. Note the stepped back notch near the bottom as on Pawnee cradleboards. Photograph courtesy Museum of the American Indian, Heye Foundation. Photograph by Carmelo Guadagno.*

11. *Ponca woman with child on cradleboard. NAA 77-8706. A four-pointed star is painted on the center panel with the hoop thong originating at the center of the star, but this example lacks standard Pawnee border design. Photograph courtesy Smithsonian Institution, National Anthropological Archives.*

12. *Wichita baby carrier, c.1900? Made from willow rods. 32" long. MAI 2/1961. Collected by M. R. Harrington in Oklahoma before 1910. Photograph courtesy Museum of the American Indian, Heye Foundation.*

13. *Wichita woman with child in baby carrier. NAA 1340. Photographed by F. A. Rinehart at the Trans-Mississippi and International Exposition at Omaha, Nebraska, 1898. Photograph courtesy Smithsonian Institution, National Anthropological Archives.*

10

11

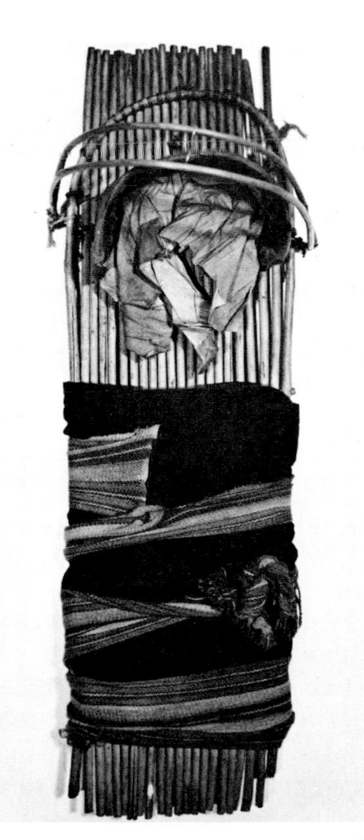

12

13

14

15

14. *Osage child in cradleboard. NAA 54,917. Note that the hoop thong originates just below the design panel. Photograph by G. W. Parsons at Pawhuska, Oklahoma, c.1890s. Photograph courtesy Smithsonian Institution, National Anthropological Archives.*

15. *Cradleboard, Osage, c.1910? Carved and painted cedar? board of milled lumber. A typical Osage design panel split into two equal vertical sections each with hourglass-like designs. Chandler-Pohrt Collection. Photograph by Dennis Lessard.*

never put on the ground, lest animals should harm it; nor was it thrown into the water, lest fishes should eat it, in which case the child would be sickly and die (Dorsey 1904b: 11).

The Pawnee most likely practiced a similar custom, although I did not record this from the Pawnee literature. The Arikara, who are also of Caddoan stock and closely related to the Pawnee, do have a very similar tradition:

> Placenta were wrapped in cloth and placed into the crotch of a tree, high enough so dogs and other animals could not reach them; they were never burned or buried (Hilger 1951).

I was unable to locate any specific mention of what type of baby carrier was utilized by the Arikara, but suspect that the Arikara baby carrier was much like that of their Mandan and Hidatsa neighbors — a tanned hide container without backboards. Bowers describes this type for the Hidatsa:

> The child was wrapped in soft tanned hide and placed in a cradle made of buffalo hide. The household group made the cradle, the men providing a young buffalo's hide which the women tanned prior to cutting and sewing the parts together (Bowers 1965: 128).

Prairie Siouan Cradleboards

Osage cradleboards are fairly common in collections, probably because the Osage continued to make them long after other tribes discontinued this practice. Osage boards are usually made of cedar, poplar, or birch; and resemble the Pawnee boards in having the top one-third decorated with a carved and painted design. They differ in that the thong holding the hoop originates just below the design area; rather than from the middle of the design area as on Pawnee boards. Osage boards also have tribally distinct designs which differ from Pawnee designs. Osage designs normally have no decorative border, but a simple solid line instead. In place of the Pawnee star designs, the Osage usually split the design panel into two vertical halves, with a common design unit being an hourglass-like element in each half (Figs. 14 and 15). Very rarely an Osage board will have some other design element, or not be split into the two equal halves; but these may represent recent atypical types. In addition, Osage boards often have a row of pierced holes just below the design section. These holes are flat on the bottom and rounded at the top. For a description of Osage cradleboards, including some star symbolism see Mathews pages 327-330.

The Osage style of cradleboard has had a fairly wide distribution and is recorded for the Iowa, Oto, and Kaw (Skinner 1926: 281). It is also the type recently made by the Pawnee, as recorded by Dr. James Howard. All of the cradleboards of the Osage type that I have seen were made of commercial lumber, and probably date from the past 100 years. It is probably a continuation of an earlier Osage tradition, most likely shared by Kaw and Quapaw who are closely related, and a recent introduction to other tribes.

According to Fletcher and La Flesche, who wrote the definitive monograph on the Omaha, the Omaha used an undecorated cradleboard without a hoop (Fletcher and La Flesche 1906). I have observed babies tied to plain boards on the Omaha Reservation in Nebraska, and boards of this type without a hoop can be seen in some old Omaha field photos. However, Dorsey in an 1896 report describes and illustrates a drawing of a cradleboard with a hoop and a decorated top section. Dorsey also mentions a fan:

> which is suspended from a bow of wood, is about six inches square, and is made of interwoven sinew on which beads have been strung. Occasionally thimbles and other bright objects dangle from the bottom of the fan (Dorsey 1896: 275-276).

Only one old example of an Omaha cradleboard could be found (Fig. 10).

The Ponca shared a common language and area with the Omaha until 1877, and they still continue to visit each other and intermarry; so their customs are basically the same. Ponca cradleboards are described as having a hoop (Zimmerman 1941: 96) and (Howard 1965: 51, 144). Fig. 11 shows a nicely decorated Ponca cradleboard with a simple four-pointed star design and the hoop thong originating in the center of the design; but it lacks the decorative borders of the typical Pawnee board. The similarity of this Ponca board to some Pawnee examples is still evident and again indicates close ties between the Pawnee and the Ponca-Omaha.

Miscellaneous Notes

Gene Weltfish mentions that the designs painted on Pawnee parfleche containers represented "cosmic symbols," and she includes a drawing of one such design (Weltfish 1965: 214-216, Figs. 27-2 and 27-3). The second illustration in Weltfish — "The significance of which is unknown" — does not appear to represent a star symbol. Mabel Morrow in her recent monograph on rawhide does not mention symbolism for the Pawnee, but she does illustrate a burden strap with a four-pointed star design (Morrow 1975: 190). It may be that the Pawnee used star symbolism on their parfleche containers at an early period, and then changed to non-symbolic geometric designs sometime before 1900. None of the documented Pawnee parfleches I have seen have apparent star symbolism.

It may be of interest to note that the painted parfleche designs of the Osage (along with other Siouan tribes) are divided into two equal vertical panels much like the typical Osage cradleboard design. The relationship of designs painted on parfleches to other designs used by the same tribe would make for an interesting study by some future scholar.

Much of the literature concerning cradleboards deals with possible side effects such as head deformation and personality changes. The literature on this subject is vast, and could form the basis for a separate article. I shall not discuss this here, but will end with a quote from Driver:

> Superficial comparison of personality in the Arctic and tropical areas of North America, where infants are not swaddled or bound to cradling devices, suggests no marked differences in adult personality between these areas and the rest of the continent. Therefore, for areas where binding is the rule, this aspect of infant treatment seems to have little to do with adult personality (Driver 1969: 454).

Author's Note

Most of the Pawnee cradleboard specimens and illustrations of Pawnee cradleboards known to me are shown with this article. The reader may be interested in a few additions to these. The Chandler-Pohrt Collection contains a small cradleboard collected by Milford Chandler from the Pawnee in Oklahoma, but it is a more recent and somewhat degenerate form in that it is painted with commercial paints and not carved.

I have seen a small cradleboard with fine carving in the museum attached to Pawnee Bill's Trading Post at Pawnee, Oklahoma. Unfortunately I neglected to get a photograph of this example and it has since been sold. Its present location is unknown to me.

There is a line drawing of a Pawnee cradleboard in Robert H. Lowie's Indians of the Plains *(New York: American Museum Science Books, The Natural History Press, 1963, Fig. 13). I have been unable to locate the source of this drawing.*

An old Pawnee, or possibly an Omaha cradleboard is shown in a photograph of Julius Meyer's Indian Store at Omaha, Nebraska, taken c.1875. This is reproduced in David R. Phillips' The West — An American Experience *(A. & W. Publishers Visual Library, 1973, p. 185).*

If any readers know of any other examples of Pawnee cradleboards in public or private collections, I would appreciate hearing about them.

Finally I would like to express my appreciation to several people who have helped by supplying photographs or information: Milford Chandler, Wendell Frantz, Peter Gibbs, James Howard, J.C.H. King, Dennis Lessard, Richard Pohrt, and Ben Stone. To each, my thanks. N.F.

Bibliography

Bowers, Alfred W.
1965 Hidatsa social and ceremonial organization. *Bureau of American Ethnology Bulletin* 194.

Curtis, Edward S.
1930 *The North American Indians,* Vol. 19. Plimpton Press, Norwood, Mass.

Curtis, Natalie
1907 *The Indian's book.* Harper & Brothers, New York.

Dellinger, S.C.
1936 Baby cradles of the Ozark Bluff-Dwellers. *American Antiquity* 1:3.

Densmore, Frances
1929 Pawnee music. *Bureau of American Ethnology Bulletin* 93.

Dorsey, George A.
1904a Traditions of the Skidi Pawnee. *Memoirs of the American Folklore Society,* Vol. 8, Boston.
1904b *The mythology of the Wichita.* Carnegie Institution of Washington, No. 21.

Dorsey, G.A. and Murie, J.R.
1940 Notes on Skidi Pawnee society. *Field Museum Anthropological Series,* Vol. 27, Chicago.

Dorsey, James O.
1896 Omaha dwellings, furniture and implements. *Bureau of American Ethnology 13th Annual Report.*

Driver, Harold E.
1969 *Indians of North America.* University of Chicago Press, Chicago.

Fletcher, A.C.
1902 Star cult among the Pawnee. *American Anthropologist,* n.s. Vol. 4.
1903 Pawnee star lore. *Journal of American Folklore,* Vol. 16.

Fletcher, A.C. and La Flesche, F.
1906 The Omaha tribe. *Bureau of American Ethnology 27th Annual Report.*

Hilger, Sister Inez
1951 Some customs relating to Arikara Indian child life. *Primitive Man* 24:4.

Howard, James H.
1965 The Ponca tribe. *Bureau of American Ethnology Bulletin 195.*

Hughes, Jack T.
1974 Prehistory of the Caddoan-speaking tribes. *Caddoan Indian,* Vol. 5. Garland Publishing New York.

Mason, Otis T.
1910 Cradles. In Handbook of American Indians north of Mexico, Vol. 1, edited by F.W. Hodge. *Bureau of American Ethnology Bulletin* 30:357-359.

Mathews, John J.
1961 *The Osage, children of the middle waters.* University of Oklahoma Press, Norman, Oklahoma.

Morrow, Mabel
1975 *Indian rawhide.* University of Oklahoma Press, Norman, Oklahoma.

Skinner, Alanson
1925 Ethnology of the Sauk, notes on material culture. *Milwaukee Public Museum Bulletin,* Vol. 5, Part 3.
1926 Ethnology of the Ioway. *Milwaukee Public Museum Bulletin,* Vol. 5, No. 4.

Spier, Leslie
1928 Havasupai ethnography. *Anthropological papers of the American Museum of Natural History,* Vol. 29, Part 3, New York (contains the best comparative discussion of cradle types for Indians west of the Great Plains).

Weltfish, Gene
1965 *The Lost Universe.* Basic Books, Inc., New York.

Zimmerman, Charles L.
1941 *White Eagle, chief of the Poncas.* Telegraph Press, Harrisburg, Penn.

Norman Feder, author of American Indian Art *(Harry N. Abrams, Inc., New York, 1969), has written extensively on many aspects of the field. For the last eighteen months he has served as special Editorial Consultant to this magazine.*

THREE EFFIGY PIPES
BY AN EASTERN DAKOTA MASTER CARVER

John C. Ewers

It was the American artist, George Catlin, who first brought to the attention of students of Indian life and customs the fact that some of the red stone pipes made by Indians of the Upper Mississippi and Upper Missouri valleys prior to the middle 1830s were "designed and carved with much taste and skill, with figures and groups in *alto relievo,* standing or reclining upon them." In his best-known book, *Letters and Notes on the Manners, Customs, and Condition of the North American Indians,* published at his own expense in London in 1841, Catlin pictured seven human effigy pipes in outline on Plate 98, even though he identified none of them by tribe of origin.

I have recently edited for publication the elaborately illustrated monograph on North American Indian tobacco pipes which George Catlin prepared for the English pipe collector, William Bragge, during the early 1860s, and which is preserved in the British Museum in London. That work reveals that prior to 1836 some Sioux and Pawnee effigy pipe carvers treated the shanks of catlinite pipes as platforms for social commentary on such matters as love, Indian attitudes toward white men, and the liquor trade.

Now I should like to present evidence that effigy pipes continued to be carved among the Eastern Dakota of the Upper Mississippi during the late 1830s and 1840s and to suggest that such carving was brought to a peak of perfection at the hand of one highly skilled Indian sculptor within that period. This evidence is offered in the form of three catlinite pipes in the collections of as many museums.

In both his British Museum manuscript and his 1841 book George Catlin pictured a Pawnee pipe with two men seated upon the shank, facing each other and struggling for the possession of a keg of liquor. Two of the pipes I now refer to also provide mute, three-dimensional comments on Indian interest in the liquor trade. That trade thrived among the tribes of the Upper Mississippi Valley during the 1830s and 1840s despite the facts that it was then unlawful to transport liquor into the Indian Country, and soldiers at Fort Snelling tried to prevent it from being smuggled up river to the villages and camps of the Sioux and Chippewa. Even so, those Indians had a strong craving for "spirit water," as they termed whiskey, and they regarded obtaining a keg or bottle of it as an achievement of which to be proud.

One catlinite pipe portrays a man seated upon a small platform atop the shank facing the smoker. He holds a small keg on his knees and between his outstretched arms. His eyes, nose, mouth, ears and long, flowing hair are carefully delineated. His barrel-chested body is realistically proportioned. His shoulders and arms are well-muscled. By contrast his legs are quite thin, his knees malformed, and his feet small. Collected by the famous French explorer of the Upper Mississippi, Joseph N. Nicollet (1786-1843), this pipe is preserved in the American Museum of Natural History, in New York, as Catalog No. 12-51 (Figs. 1,2). This may have been one of the "calumets" Nicollet wrote that he was taking back to Baltimore with him along with "pebbles, plants, birds,

1,2. *Front and side views of a human figure holding a keg on his knees, carved on a lead-inlaid catlinite pipe. Collected by Joseph N. Nicollet, c.1837. The American Museum of Natural History, New York, Cat. No. 12-51.*

reptiles, quadrupeds, medicine bags, and moccasins," in a letter he addressed to Henry H. Sibley from the Ohio River steamboat, Maryland, and dated November 27, 1837.

A second and more elaborate effigy pipe presents two men facing one another on a platform atop the shank (Figs. 3,4). The larger of the two men must have been intended to be a chief, for he wears a medal suspended from a cord around his neck. He is seated on the platform at a low, four-legged table and holds a bottle with his right hand. His left hand is broken off. It might have held a glass or cup. Facing the chief and grasping two legs of the table with his outstretched hands is a smaller male figure carved in the round from a little below the waist up. Presumably he is waiting to receive some of the coveted liquor in a cup or glass or perhaps even as a swig directly from the chief's bottle.

There can be little doubt that the figures on this pipe were carved by the same sculptor who created the man with the keg on his knees on the pipe previously described. They are very nearly the same size, the larger of the two figures on the second pipe being very little over two inches high. The treatment of the features of the head and hair, the well-developed upper body and well-muscled arms are alike. So are the thin legs, peculiarly arched knees, and small feet of the seated figures.

This pipe was part of the old War Department Collection which was transferred to the National Institute in the Patent Office in Washington in 1841. During the late '50s it was transferred again, this time to the Smithsonian Institution, where it was catalogued in 1867 as No. 2,622 from the "Valley of the Missouri River." A poorly detailed drawing of this pipe was published at the top of Plate 69 of Vol. II of Henry Rowe Schoolcraft's *Historical and Statistical Information Respecting the History, Condition and Prospects of the Indian Tribes of the United States* (1854), where the pipe was identified as of Dakota origin.

Still a third catlinite pipe which should be attributed to the same unnamed Indian sculptor is pictured in Fig. 5. On the platform atop the pipe shank sits a single Indian man, with legs apart and bent at the knees, and small feet like the seated men on the other two pipes. He faces the smoker, with his arms outstretched and the palm of one hand on each knee. Although his head is shaved, save for the suggestion of a crest at the top, his facial features, heavy chest and well-muscled arms, as well as his thin legs closely resemble those of the seated men on the other pipes. Observe also that all four human figures carved on these pipes wear no clothing other than a broad belt about the waist rendered by carving in relief. This third pipe is Cat. No. 10,401 in the Museum für Völkerkunde in Vienna. Collected in the vicinity of St. Paul, Minnesota, in 1853 by a man named Scherzer, this pipe was attributed to the "Eastern Dakota?" by Christian Feest in his excellent catalogue of the North American Indian Collection in the Museum für Völkerkunde, Vienna. (There illustrated as Item 169, Plate vii, and described on page 89.)

Although the painstakingly carved realistic human figures are probably the most interesting features of these three pipes, their similarities in style are not the only design features common to these pipes. Two of the three pipes have very realistically carved heads and foreparts of animals carved on their prows — one a dog, the other a bear. It is very obvious, too, that the unnamed pipe maker who created these pipes was very fond of decorating both the upright bowl portions and the stem ends of the shanks with geometric designs in lead inlay. On the sides of the shanks of all three of these pipes appears the same geometric inlaid design ending in a form somewhat suggestive of an animal's hoof.

Unfortunately, we do not know the name of the superb Indian artist and craftsman who fashioned these effigy pipes during the second quarter of the nineteenth century. He was most probably a member of one of the Eastern Dakota or Santee Sioux divisions, who was actively engaged in pipe-making over an extended period of years prior to 1853. The quality of his work, as represented by these three pipes preserved in three widely separated museums, readily identifies him as a master worker in catlinite who combined a love of elaborate geometric ornament in lead inlay with a remarkable talent for carving small, delicately detailed, human and animal forms from parts of solid blocks of red pipestone from the famous quarry in southwestern Minnesota. Surely he must have possessed infinite patience to be able to produce such elaborately conceived works, and he must have learned from experience how fine a miniature arm or leg he could carve in brittle stone without breaking and spoiling one of his masterworks. It would seem extremely improbable that these were the only pipes this master carved, even though

3,4. *Side view and detail of two human figures illustrating the distribution of liquor by a chief, carved on a lead-inlaid catlinite pipe. 7¾" long. From the old War Department Collection, transferred to The National Institute in 1841. National Museum of Natural History, Washington, D.C., Cat. No. 2,622.*

5. *View of a seated human figure with hands on knees, carved on a lead-inlaid catlinite pipe. 6¾" long. Collected by a man named Scherzer near St. Paul in 1853. Museum für Völkerkunde, Vienna, Cat. No. 10,401.*

they may be the only ones known to have been preserved.

We cannot know why this master carver created these elaborate pipes. But it is possible that even as long as 140 or more years ago this Indian sculptor, who lived beyond the frontier of white settlement at that time, was creating his masterpieces for sale to palefaced collectors. We now know that during his travels on the Upper Mississippi and Missouri in the years 1830-1836 George Catlin met several fur traders, Indian agents, and Army officers who owned collections of effigy pipes carved by talented Indian artists from that bright red stone that was later to be named catlinite in Catlin's honor.

Among these collectors were two very prominent Indian agents then employed by the War Department which was in charge of Indian Affairs for the federal government. General William Clark, famed co-leader of the Lewis and Clark Expedition overland to the Pacific Ocean, had become Superintendent of Indian Affairs in St. Louis. As early as 1816 he built a large addition to his home on the St. Louis waterfront to serve as both a council room for meeting visiting Indian delegations and as the first museum west of the Mississippi. His extensive Indian collections displayed in that room included a number of effigy pipes. Another collector of these pipes was Major Lawrence Taliaferro who in 1820 began eighteen years of successful service as agent to the Upper Mississippi tribes, which included both the Eastern Dakota and Ojibwa. In 1820 also, construction was started on a large military post overlooking the Mississippi River some eight miles below the Falls of St. Anthony. Three years later steamboat service was inaugurated between St. Louis and that post, which soon thereafter became known as Fort Snelling. Fort Snelling served as more than a military post and headquarters for the Indian agent in charge of the Upper Mississippi tribes. It also became a center for the marketing of Indian arts and crafts such as the colorful, carved tobacco pipes of the Eastern Dakota.

Pipes continued on page 74

THE ARTISTRY AND GENIUS OF
JULIUS CAESAR

Rosemary Ellison

Julius Caesar, master metalsmith, was born on March 20, 1910, in Pawnee, Oklahoma. During the past forty years, his career as a smith has been unusual and inspiring — a remarkable story of self-development, personal research, and a variety of business experiences. He has achieved artistic concepts and standards which make him one of the most creative metalsmiths in the United States today. Caesar learned his craft through apprenticeship under two metalsmiths, both of whom are now deceased. A member of the Pawnee Indian tribe, Caesar was first introduced to metalwork in the 1930s by serving as an apprentice to Hiram Jake, a Pawnee metalsmith who specialized in jewelry related to the Native American Church.

> ". . . When I first started this work, I used to watch one man, his name was Hiram Jake and he was viewed as an outstanding metal craftsman in the field of peyote religion jewelry. I watched him, his techniques, his tools and all that. He had some boys and his boys weren't interested in metalwork and having a lifelong interest in carrying on the tradition of metalwork, he said to me, 'Brother, it's a shame that my children won't take any interest in this; it's a growing field, someday for the Pawnees. I'll be willing to teach you and give you some knowledge of what these symbols mean'. . ."

Through the inspiration and guidance of Hiram Jake, Caesar became fascinated with German silver, a metal of European derivation which has been widely used by Southern Plains Indians since the 1850s. German silver, also known as nickel silver, is a nonferrous alloy of copper, nickel and zinc.

Another important experience in Julius Caesar's early training was the instruction received from his father-in-law, Bill Leaf, a Sac and Fox metalsmith from Tama, Iowa. Bill Leaf helped Caesar to further his knowledge and understanding of Woodlands-style metalwork. Many of the tools Caesar uses in his work once belonged to Bill Leaf.

Julius Caesar is unique in his exploration, research, and mastery of a wide variety of Indian metalwork styles. From the early 1950s through the early 1960s, Caesar undertook extensive travels in order to promote and sell his work as well as to observe and record new forms of metalwork. Caesar maintained a notebook in which he systematically recorded the many tribal variations in designs and symbols. Through his travels and tribal contacts, Caesar gained tremendous firsthand experience which would provide the basis for his later creative achievements. In discussing his early research efforts with him, one discovers that he has perceived an incredible range of regional differences and types of products.

In his travels, Caesar often visited museums where he was able to study examples of pre-Columbian and historic metalwork produced by the native peoples of North America. Caesar made detailed sketches which he later utilized in his own design work. In his travels to new areas, Caesar explored the traditional styles of metalwork by talking to individuals and searching for as many "old" examples as possible in order to reconstruct his own version

1. *Pin, late 1968-early 1969, 2⅞"L.* **2.** *Neckerchief slide, 1974, 3⅛"L.* **3.** *Linked earrings, 1968, 7¼"L.* **4.** *Neckerchief slide, 1974, 4⅛"L.* **5.** *Pendant with ball and cone dangles, 1971, 7¼"L x 3⅞"w. All nickel silver.*

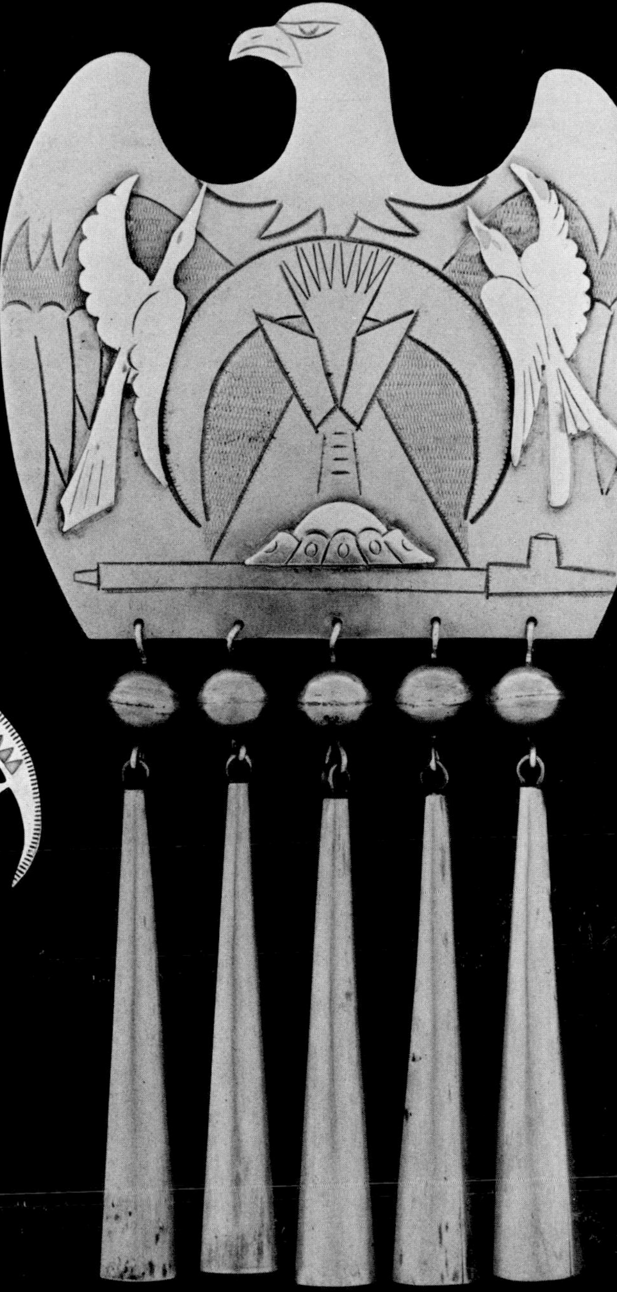

1

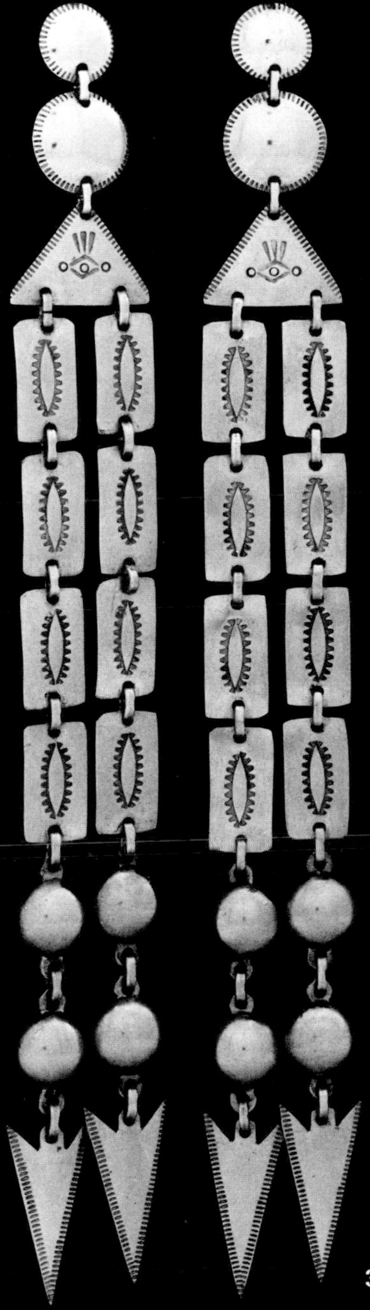

5

3

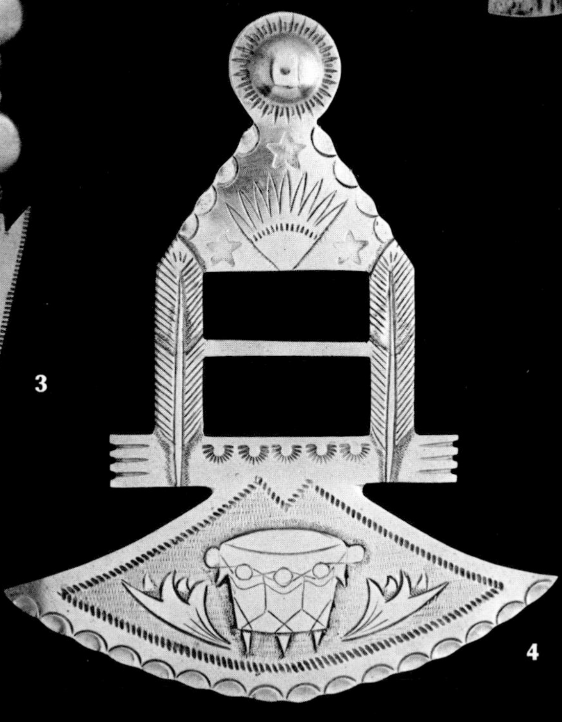

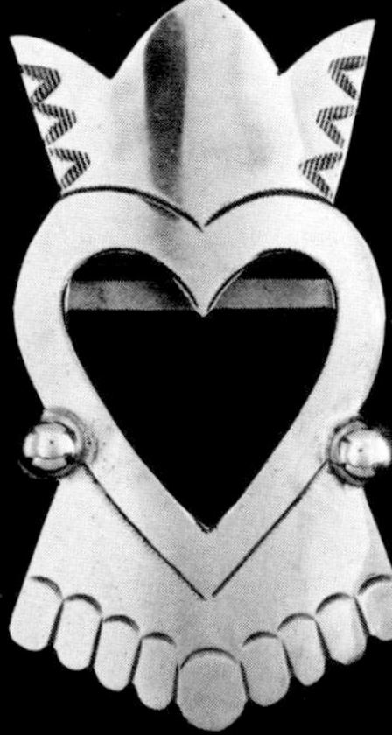

2

4

of the original tribal style. Often, while gathering information, Caesar would discover a living metalsmith still producing within the tribal group. Learning this, he would visit the craftsman and attempt to obtain his records. Usually he was successful, and many times the metalsmith would permit Caesar to have his designs as well as examples of his jewelry. Over the years Caesar built up his own collection of metalwork which he used to teach his sons.

In 1963-64, Caesar established a mail-order business in Marshalltown, Iowa, and issued an illustrated catalogue which reflected his wide knowledge of tribal design. Marshalltown was an ideal base of operations for Caesar because its central location allowed him to make frequent trips to the Great Lakes region, to Kansas, Nebraska and the Dakotas, as well as to Oklahoma and Texas. During his numerous trips to the Chicago area, Caesar frequently met and talked with Iroquois Indians from New York and Canada. Learning that there were so few smiths among the Iroquois, Caesar took every opportunity to find out as much as possible about the early styles. Although the symbolism was admittedly new to him, Caesar nevertheless gained more than enough knowledge to undertake the re-creation of traditional forms of Iroquois metalwork to fill increasing orders from Iroquois tribesmen. Approaching an unfamiliar style of metalwork with consummate respect for its significance within Iroquoian culture, Caesar points out that Iroquois people recognize each other through the distinctive symbols of their jewelry.

Julius Caesar's background of knowledge is a vast compilation of his research endeavors, tribal contacts and various business experiences. The backbone of it all is his broad knowledge of various tribal styles. After seeing and/or acquiring the finest examples possible, Caesar brought his own creative talents into play, producing contemporary metalwork jewelry appealing to a particular tribal group. Through the acceptance of special commission work for individuals and institutions, Caesar continually demonstrated his ability to duplicate traditional tribal styles as specified or to broaden and embellish a basic tribal design, refining it until the finished piece was a unique contemporary creation.

Well versed in the history and culture of many tribal groups, Caesar is aware of his significant role in preserving and maintaining Indian culture through his contemporary metalwork creations.

"... A symbolic piece whatever it may be, a pendant with tribal symbols perhaps, I develop it from an old-fashioned style into a contemporary piece, I modernize it ..."

While the scope of Julius Caesar's achievements in German silver is vast, his forte is Plains Indian style metalwork with special emphasis on jewelry related to the religious rites of the Native American Church.

The Native American Church of North America was originally organized by adherents of the Peyote Cult who incorporated to express their religious beliefs. Membership in the church is intertribal and it is chartered in some states. The practice of peyote ceremonialism is primarily one of prayer and quiet contemplation. Ritual practices of the church involve ingestion of the sacramental peyote, accompanied by prayers and songs, during an all-night ceremony usually held in a tipi. In relation to the art of German silver metalwork, the Peyote Cult brought about the development of unique designs representing the iconography of the Native American Church. A special style of jewelry, commonly referred to as "peyote jewelry," has been created and is ornamented with or made in the form of iconographic symbols of the Native American Church. Foremost of importance in church symbolism is the sacred waterbird to whom the prayers of the worshippers are entrusted. It is the most common religious symbol found in peyote jewelry, and is usually depicted with neck and wings as if in flight. Peyote jewelry is commonly worn outside of its religious context, offering highly stylized graceful forms for personal wear.

Julius Caesar is one of the most imaginative creators of Native American Church jewelry at work today. Especially inspired by the symbolism of the sacred waterbird, Caesar has designed and created a multitude of waterbird designs for earrings, stickpins and other types of jewelry.

Caesar was among the first to recognize the emerging importance of the Native American Church among the Woodlands tribes. His acute business sensitivities alerted him to the marketing opportunities at hand as he quickly introduced Native American Church jewelry items to Woodlands tribesmen. The overall impact of Caesar's endeavors proved to be a tremendous influence on many other craftsmen who "adopted" many of his designs for use in their own work.

As with the sacred waterbird, the varied

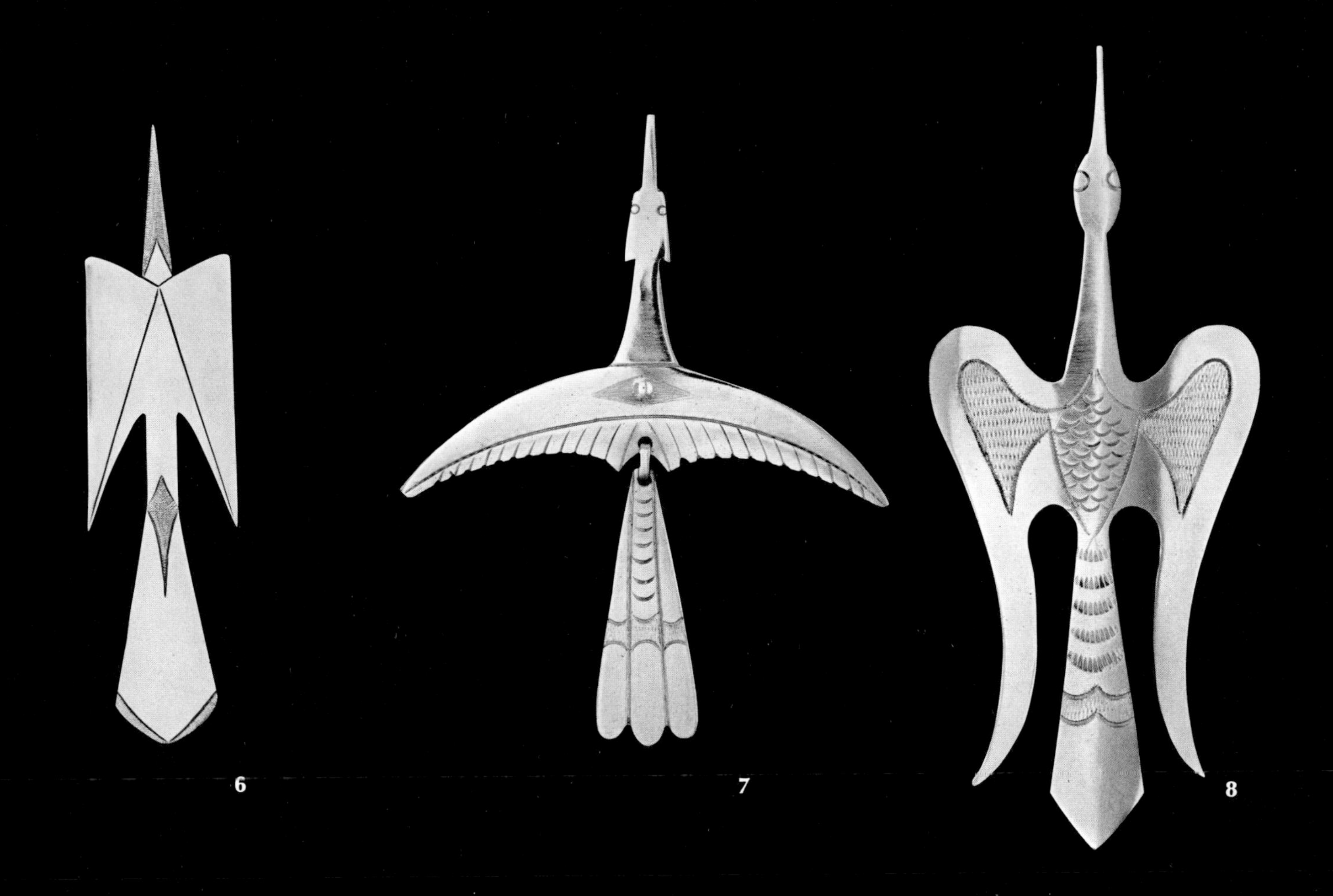

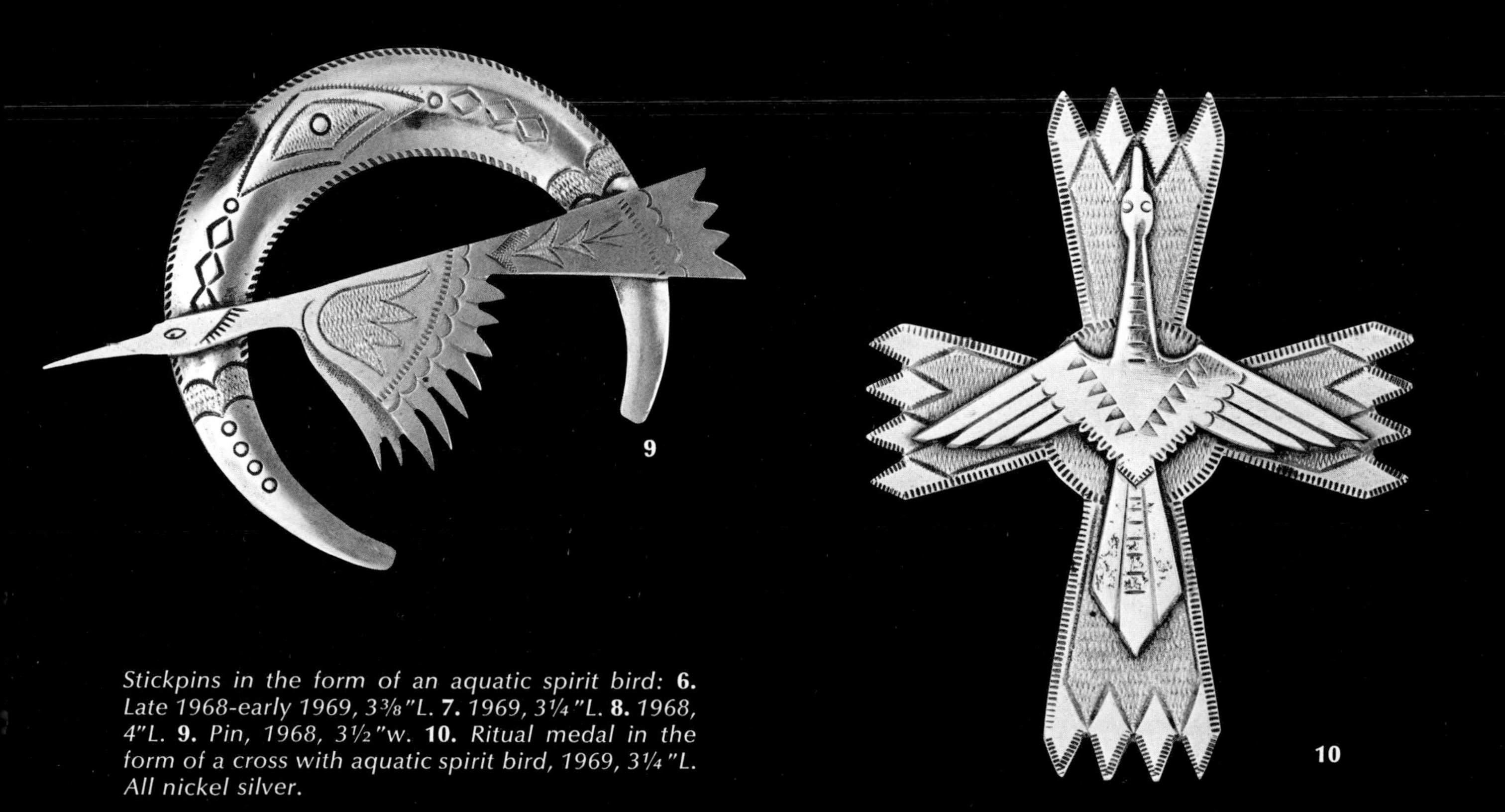

Stickpins in the form of an aquatic spirit bird: **6.** *Late 1968-early 1969, 3⅜"L.* **7.** *1969, 3¼"L.* **8.** *1968, 4"L.* **9.** *Pin, 1968, 3½"w.* **10.** *Ritual medal in the form of a cross with aquatic spirit bird, 1969, 3¼"L. All nickel silver.*

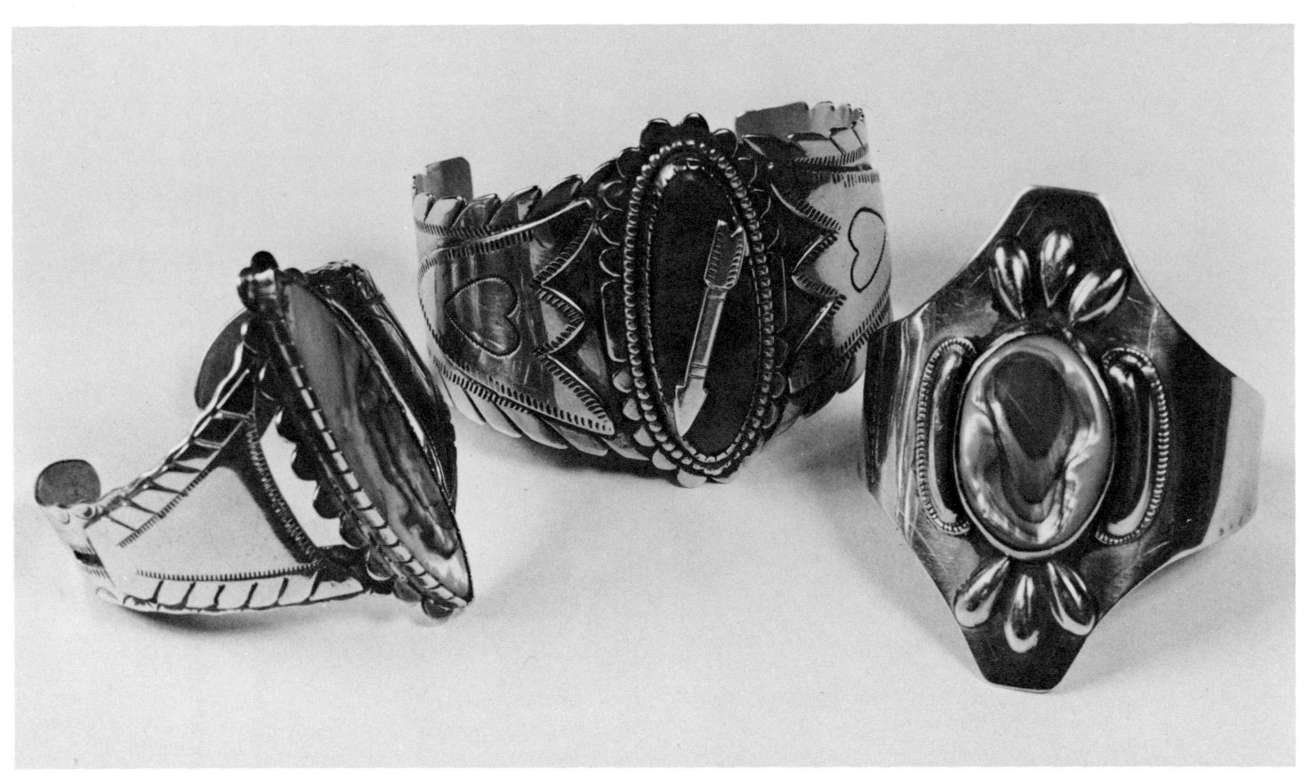

11. *Bracelets, 1978. Nickel silver with abalone shell (left and right), polished agate (center). Diameters, ½", 2¾", 2¼". Left and center in Woodlands style, right derived from Southwest design. All photographs illustrating this article courtesy of the United States Department of the Interior, Indian Arts and Crafts Board, Southern Plains Indian Museum and Crafts Center.*

symbolism of religious concepts growing out of Native American Church beliefs provides artistic inspiration for the creation of a considerable amount of art, particularly in the Southern Plains region. Julius Caesar feels quite protective of the beliefs and doctrines of the church, having stated,

"... German silver symbolism of the Native American order has meaning just for an Indian, it's not for the white man to know ..."

However, many of the designs can be read within a Christian context that is entirely compatible with Native American beliefs. Jewelry pieces incorporating a heart as part of the design refer to the compassion of Christ's sacrifice, while other symbolic references such as the crescent altar shape, the peyote button and feather fans are more obscure to the nonmember.

Julius Caesar is a proud yet humble man, keenly aware of his capabilities as well as his limitations. Typically, he rises at 2:00 a.m. to begin his working day, filling orders for special commission work which he continues to receive from throughout the United States, although he is now unofficially "retired" from his business. Time has always been very valuable to him, or as he puts it, "... there's no need to be in bed, when I wake, I'm awake ..."

While pointing out that, "... German silver is cheap but it has certainly served its purpose ...," Caesar is often defensive in describing his preference for nickel silver but his arguments in favor of the metal are indicative of his commitment to working in this medium Caesar states that nickel silver is one of the hardest, most difficult metals to work with. It is extremely difficult to engrave, but Caesar prefers it to sterling silver which he feels is not only too expensive but presents relatively little challenge as a medium,

"... Now, that sterling, there isn't much to it as far as putting designs on it. You don't have to use much weight to indent your designs. If you make mistakes, you can rub them out and start over. You can't do that with German silver ..."

In discussing why German silver metalwork is relatively little-known, Caesar points out that one of the reasons is that production of a large quantity of metalwork for sale is difficult because so much handwork is involved. A metalsmith working in nickel silver is not capable of producing a large quantity of work unless some power equipment is used. Caesar feels that power equipment is essential in his jewelry production because it saves him time. Primarily, he relies upon three types of machinery: saws, a metal punch for cutting out circles, and lapidary machines for cutting and polishing stone and shell. Caesar feels that anytime he can use a machine to reduce the amount of handwork required, he is ahead. On the other hand, he is quite disdainful of contemporary metalsmiths who make use of handpresses to stamp out their work mechanically.

Keenly interested in protecting his work, Caesar developed the first hallmark to be used by a contemporary metalsmith working in nickel silver. He is particularly concerned about misrepresentation of his work by non-Indians. He has proudly refused monetary offers to reveal the secrets of his trade stating,

> . . . "That's my soul, that metalcraft that I'm doing, it's my knowledge from all the years I took to gather research for my own personal use and needs . . ."

Realizing how other Indian people have helped him in the past, Caesar has unselfishly provided instruction and encouragement to many aspiring metalsmiths of Indian descent. His philosophy regarding the teaching of his art to other Indians is that these people are his friends and he is helping them accordingly,

> ". . . I'll tell them, 'Look, I'm going to permit you to use this design for the good of God. I'm a believer in God, you know, and this might bring you some good' . . ."

Caesar has always been highly motivated to promote not only his own craft, but the entire field of Indian arts and crafts. He is a member of the Oklahoma Indian Arts and Crafts Cooperative, an organization comprised of more than fifty outstanding Native American artists and craftspersons. Caesar points with pride to the fact that the Cooperative management has always been supportive of the efforts of metalsmiths working exclusively in German silver. In 1976, through a grant from the National Endowment for the Arts, the Oklahoma Indian Arts and Crafts Cooperative published the first major exhibition catalogue devoted exclusively to German silver metalwork. This publication features Julius Caesar's work with illustrations of some of his masterpieces. Caesar's interest in promoting the entire field of Native American metalwork in nickel silver led him and several other metalsmiths to cooperate with the Southern Plains Indian Museum and the Oklahoma Indian Arts and Crafts Cooperative in the organization of the exhibition, "Contemporary Southern Plains Indian Metalwork." This exhibit grew out of a series of special exhibitions at the Southern Plains Indian Museum and Crafts Center, Anadarko, Oklahoma, one of which was devoted exclusively to Caesar's metalwork.

Julius Caesar has two sons, Bruce and Harry, both of whom are metalsmiths. Bruce Caesar learned the art of metalwork at seven and turned professional four years later. Working independently out of his home, Bruce Caesar is currently devoting his entire energies to the production of custom-designed nickel silver metalwork. In sharp contrast to the prevailing marketing demands which his father experienced during the early days of his career, Bruce Caesar estimates that sixty percent of his customers are non-Indians.

Harry Caesar lives with his wife, Cecilia, in Pawnee, Oklahoma, where he works with his father. Within a short time, Harry hopes to be managing a retail shop-studio in his father's home. Julius Caesar is extremely proud of the accomplishments of both his sons, who are helping to perpetuate the Caesar reputation for excellence in metalwork.

Although Caesar has researched and recorded historic examples of metalwork and has produced older designs requested by Indian customers, his most creative accomplishment is that he has used his broad knowledge and mastery of significant symbols and styles of workmanship in creating contemporary and innovative designs which are as beautiful in appearance as they are instinctively tribal in inspiration. As a result, Julius Caesar has developed the tradition of Indian metalwork into a modern, individual accomplishment.

Bibliography

Douglas, Frederic H.

1941 *Main types of Indian metal jewelry*. The Denver Art Museum, Leaflet 104, Denver.

1950 *The Peyote Cult: ritual equipment*. The Denver Art Museum, Leaflet 106, Denver.

Douglas, Frederic H. and Alice Marriott

1942 *Metal jewelry of the Peyote Cult*. The Denver Art Museum, Material Culture Note 17, Denver.

Ellison, Rosemary

1967 *Contemporary Plains and Woodlands metalwork in German silver*. Indian Arts and Crafts Board of the United States Department of the Interior (Smoke Signals, No. 52 Spring, pp. 3-26), Washington, D.C.

Caesar continued on page 75

I. *Horse racing of Sioux Indians near Fort Pierre (after Bodmer). Chandler-Pohrt Collection.*

PLAINS INDIAN RIDING QUIRTS
WITH ELK ANTLER HANDLES

Richard A. Pohrt

The acquisition of the horse had a tremendous impact on the culture of the Plains Indians. Their methods of hunting, style of warfare, mode of travel, the dwellings they lived in, and their standards of wealth and prestige were all dramatically changed as they adapted to a new way of life centered around the horse. The introduction of the horse also had a marked effect upon the arts and crafts of these people. Horse trappings were initially influenced by the Spaniards. However, the Indian was quick to develop his own equipment and riding gear from available native materials. With the exception of iron bits, he succeeded admirably. Although horse gear was often spare for the war trail or hunt, elaborate trappings were developed for social occasions. The distinctive regalia used to outfit the horse made an impressive sight. The Indian created decorated saddles, saddle blankets, martingales, cruppers, headstalls, and other accoutrements which are objects of great beauty. These horse trappings play an important part in presenting the Plains Indians as one of the most colorful and picturesque groups the world has known.

One of the interesting items to emerge from the association of Indians with the horse was the riding whip or quirt. I prefer to use the term *quirt* since its meaning is more precise. The quirt, made and used by equestrian Indians, may be described as a short riding whip consisting of a handle, wrist strap, and lash. The handle was generally made of elk antler or wood; the wrist strap of native tanned leather, occasionally decorated with beads of porcupine quillwork; and the lash of buffalo hide or harness leather.

The purpose of the quirt was to urge a horse to move quickly in the hunt or on the war trail. However, it was not restricted to this use. It was often used by mounted warriors to "count coup" in combat. To strike an enemy in battle with the hand or an object held in the hand was a deed that rated high in the order of war honors. Soldier bands might use their quirts on fellow tribesmen to enforce camp rules. James Willard Schultz, a writer of adventure stories for boys based on his experiences with the Blackfeet, records such uses of the quirt.

"Eight of the Seizers firmly held him while others hurried to get possession of his weapons, and still others took up every piece of the fat meat we had brought in. As soon as this was done, the Chief of the Seizers advanced and struck my father upon the back with a riding-quirt. It was not a hard blow, but the broad rawhide lashes made a loud spat when they hit the soft and tightly stretched leather shirt he wore. Some of the people groaned at the sound of it . . . again and again, six strokes in all, the quirt lashes spatted against my father's back, but he did not flinch and made no outcry" (Schultz 1918:7).

Such treatment was intended to humiliate the wrongdoer publicly, not to inflict physical pain. However, resistance might mean death.

Our attention in this article is focused on those quirts with elk antler handles. This material was probably preferred for quirt handles in the pre-reservation days. It was strong, durable, and could be obtained without difficulty over a vast area. Easy to work, it could be shaped and finished with simple tools. Any section of antler of suitable length and shape might be used. There was some preference for the prongs that protrude forward on each side of the main rack just above the skull. Relatively straight and with a slight upturn near the end, these prongs could be made into handles with a minimum of effort (Fig. 7).

The use of elk antler quirts appears to be widespread. They were probably made and used by all of the tribes of the Plains, Prairies, and Plateau. Examples from each of these areas show identical construction features. To attach the lash, a hole or cavity was bored up into the lower end of the handle. A small hole was then drilled through the antler from side to side so that it intersected the cavity. A wood or antler pin was inserted to hold the lash in place. Near the opposite end another hole was drilled for the wrist strap. This similarity of construction makes accurate tribal identification difficult or impossible. Reliable collection history may be of help in determining who made the specimen. A beaded or porcupine quilled wrist strap could provide an important clue.

II. *Crow Chiefs, Crow Indian Reservation, Montana, 1881. Photographer Frank Jay Haynes. Standing: Stand-On-The-Cloud, Crane-In-The-Sky. Seated: Medicine Crow, White-Hair-On-Temple and Bird-On-The-Ground. Note the elk antler quirt handle decorated with brass upholstery tacks held by Bird-On-The-Ground. Photograph courtesy Haynes Foundation, Bozeman, Montana.*

The quirt was a strictly utilitarian object, but this did not preclude artistic decoration. Brass upholstery tacks, a popular trade item, were sometimes used to ornament a quirt handle. A splendid example appears in the photograph of Crow Chiefs taken by F. Jay Haynes (Fig **II**). Those specimens with engraved decorations are of great interest. A variety of themes appear such as life figures, war exploits, and curvilinear and geometric patterns. An inspection of the engraved examples illustrated suggests the use of an awl or a knife point to produce fine shallow lines. Deeper lines appear to be made with the cutting edge of a knife blade or a file. Where larger areas of surface

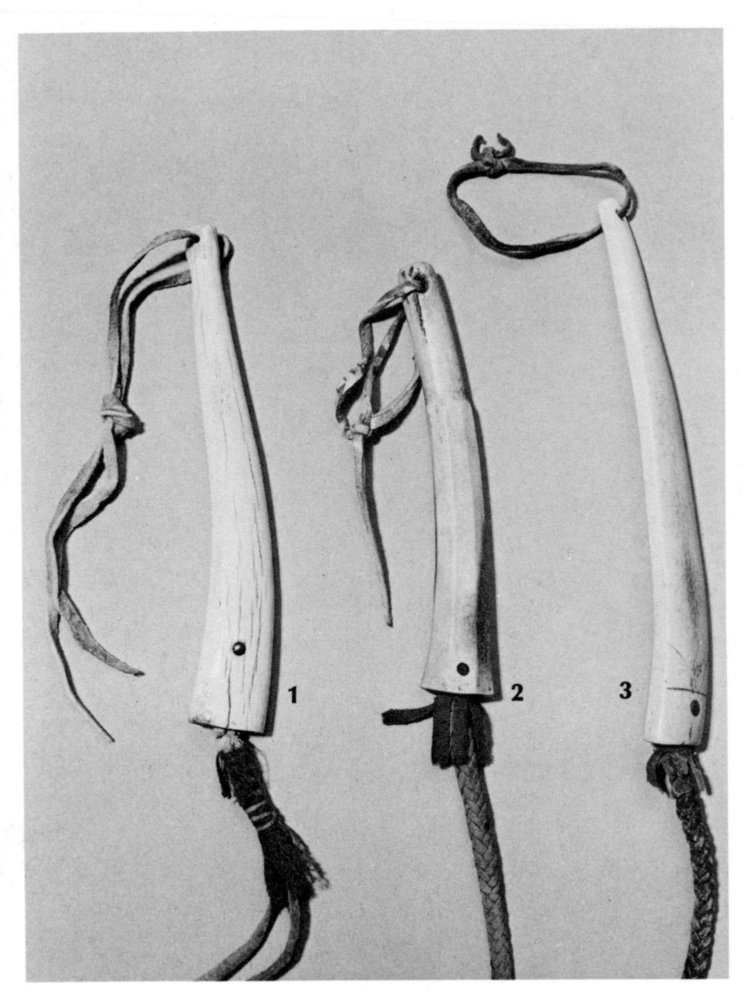
1
2
3

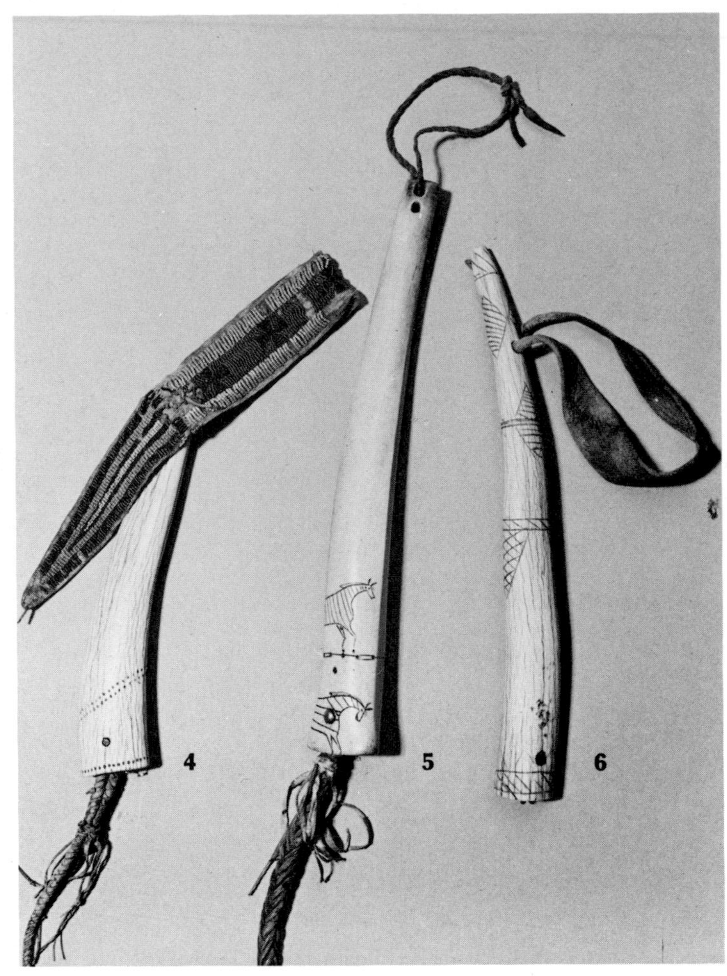
4
5
6

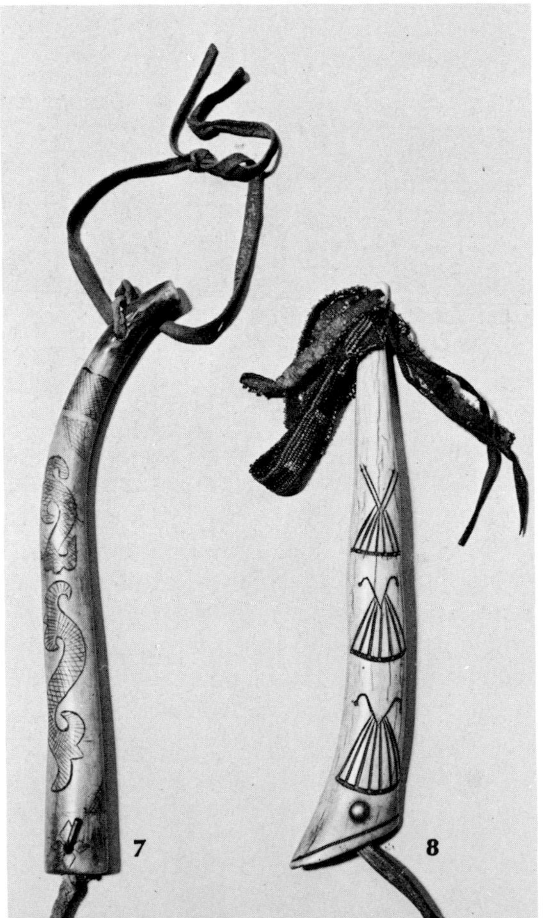
7
8

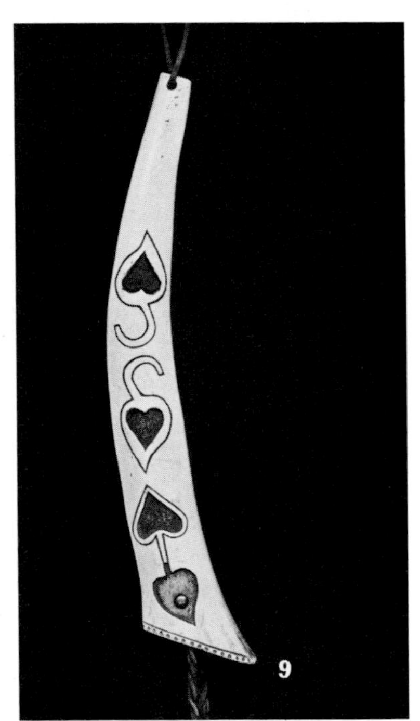
9

1. *Sioux, c.1870. Handle 30 cm, lash 47.5 cm. Smooth, polished, undecorated surface. Wood lash pin with brass upholstery tack driven into each end. Lash buffalo leather; red wool cloth fringe. Collected from member of Sitting Bull's band. Chandler-Pohrt Collection 213.*

2. *Eastern Sioux, c.1870. Handle 25.5 cm, lash 57 cm. Shaped and polished. Rounded upper section, eight-sided lower section. Wood lash pin. Lash native tanned leather with red trade cloth fringe. Chandler-Pohrt Collection 2778.*

3. *Tribe unknown, c.1860. Handle 33.4 cm, lash 33.5 cm. Flattened, squared edges; three engraved lines on reverse side. Wood lash pin. Braided lash native tanned leather. Pohrt Collection.*

4. *Sioux, c.1870. Handle 26.5 cm, lash 52.5 cm. Thickness reduced, surface polished. Red pigment rubbed into rows of dots. Wood lash pin. Lash native tanned leather. Wrist strap decorated with yellow, red, turquoise, navy blue beads. Chandler-Pohrt Collection 2140.*

5. *Sioux, c.1860. Handle 38.6 cm, lash 60 cm. Engraved with portions of horses. 23 brass nails driven into one side. Wood lash pin with brass upholstery tack driven into each end. Braided lash buffalo leather. On reverse side is old paper sticker stating "Horn handle quirt stolen from Red Cloud's camp, Black Hills, Dakota." Chandler-Pohrt Collection 2288.*

6. *Sioux (?) 1865. Handle 36.3 cm. Simple engraved line work, cross-hatching with red paint rubbed into the lines. Wood lash pin. Fragment of lash commercial harness leather; wrist strap native tanned buffalo leather. Pohrt Collection.*

7. *Sac-Fox, c.1850. Handle 28.5 cm, lash 83.3 cm. Polished, decorated surface. Cross-hatching within engraved curvilinear design. Lash pin iron nail. Lash native tanned leather. Collected at Tama, Iowa, by Milford G. Chandler. Chandler-Pohrt Collection 2785.*

8. *Sac-Fox, c.1850. Handle 29 cm, lash 56.4 cm. Deep, engraved, fan or tepee design on polished surface. Wood lash pin with brass upholstery tack driven into each end. Lash commercial harness leather. Wrist strap native tanned deerskin, decorated with red, yellow, black, pink, blue beads. Collected at Tama, Iowa, by Milford G. Chandler. Chandler-Pohrt Collection 2788.*

9. *Tribe unknown, c.1870. Handle 38.8 cm, lash 45 cm. Decoration on both sides nearly identical; designs typical Prairie. Unusually deep, large areas of antler surface removed to create designs; red and blue paint rubbed into depressed areas. Wood lash pin with brass upholstery tack driven into each end. Braided lash native tanned buffalo leather. University of Michigan Museum of Anthropology 15545.*

antler have been removed, a chisel or chisel-like tool was probably used.

Riding quirts did not go unnoticed by early visitors to the Plains. Travelers mention them in their journals and artists recorded examples in their sketches and paintings. Prince Maximilian on his journey up the Missouri River in 1833-34 observed, "In general, every Blackfoot carries a whip as well as weapons in his hand" (Ewers 1955:97). Quirts appear in the works of George Catlin, Karl Bodmer, Rudolph Friederich Kurz, Alfred Jacob Miller and others. Several of George Catlin's paintings show a man with a quirt hanging from his wrist. In his portrait of Kee-O-Kuk on horseback, the Sauk and Fox leader carries a quirt with what appears to be an elk antler handle. Perhaps it is the very one collected from Kee-O-Kuk in 1832 and now in the National Museum of Natural History in Washington, D.C. (Cat. No. 167.149). Catlin's painting of the Comanche Chief Ish-A-Ro-Yeh clearly illustrates another quirt. In the Karl Bodmer *Picture Atlas* are five plates in which quirts are visible. In "Horse Racing of Sioux Indians Near Fort Pierre" the three contestants are dramatically depicted quirting their horses (Fig. 1). In "Indian Utensils and Arms" it is obvious that Bodmer's model for the quirt he drew had an elk antler handle that was ornamented with engraved designs.

The later romantic painters of the West also included the quirt as an important accessory of the Plains Indian horseman. Frederic Remington shows quirts in a number of his sketches and paintings of mounted Indians. It is startling to note the frequency with which Charles M. Russell included them in his work. With artists and illustrators up to the present, the quirt continues to be one of the hallmarks associated with the Indian horsemen of our Western Plains.

Riding quirts are not common in most museums or private collections. This is surprising when we consider the probability that every Plains, Prairie, and Plateau Indian whose culture was so involved with the horse, had at least one quirt during his lifetime. Of those quirts that have survived, the number with fine decorated handles is small. The beautifully polished surface of the elk antler was an invitation for decoration that the Indian artist found irresistible. The engraved designs and life figures are often superb expressions of the talents of the maker. They are examples of high artistic merit, deserving a place with the best representations of Plains Indian art.

Bibliography

Bodmer, Karl
1970 *Picture atlas: travel to the Indians of the Upper Missouri 1832-34.* Herman Bender, Frankfurt/M, Germany.

Bell, Michael
1973 *Braves and buffalo: Plains Indian life in 1837. Watercolors of Alfred J. Miller.* University of Toronto Press, Toronto.

Catlin, George
1841 *Letters and notes on the manner, customs and conditions of the North American Indians.* Wiley and Putnam, New York.

Ewers, John C.
1955 The horse in Blackfoot Indian culture. *Bureau of American Ethnology,* Bulletin 159. Smithsonian Institution, Washington, D.C.

Hassrick, Peter H.
1973 *Frederic Remington.* Harry N. Abrams, Inc., New York.

Kurz, Rudolph Friederich
1937 Journal of Rudolph Friederich Kurz, edited by J.N.B. Hewitt, translated by Myrtis Jarrell. *Bureau of American Ethnology,* Bulletin 115. Smithsonian Institution, Washington, D.C.

McCracken, Harold
1957 *The Charles M. Russell book.* Doubleday & Co. Inc., New York.
1966 *The Frederic Remington book.* Doubleday & Co. Inc., New York.

Renner, Frederic G.
1966 *Charles M. Russell paintings, drawings and sculpture in the Amon G. Carter Collection.* The University of Texas Press, Austin.

Roe, Frank Gilbert
1955 *The Indian and the horse.* University of Oklahoma Press, Norman.

Schultz, James Willard
1918 *Lone Bull's mistake.* Grosset & Dunlap, New York.

Tilden, Freeman
1964 *Following the frontier with F. Jay Haynes.* Alfred A. Knopf, New York.

Wilson, Gilbert L.
1924 The horse and dog in Hidatsa culture. *Anthropological Papers of the American Museum of Natural History,* Vol. XV, New York.

The photographs accompanying this article were taken by Joseph Zayac.

A lifetime collector and student of historic Plains and Great Lakes Indian material, Richard A. Pohrt is research associate of the Cranbrook Institute of Science. He owns and operates the Great Lakes Indian Museum, Cross Village, Michigan, during the summer months.

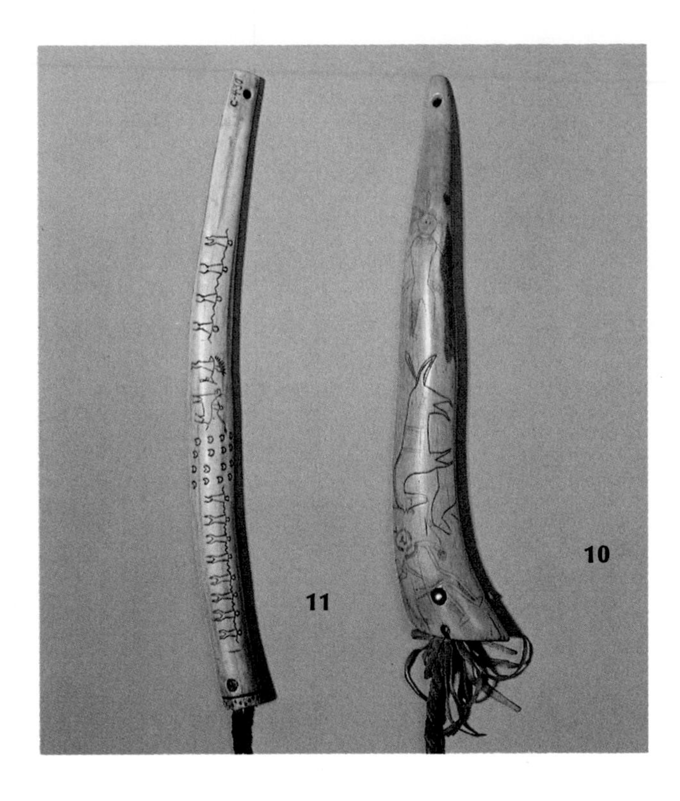

10. *Osage, c.1850. Handle 33.5 cm, lash 52.3 cm. Detailed engravings suggest pictographs. One surface shows two horses, one being held by man wearing grizzly bear claw necklace and carrying tomahawk; another man is holding tomahawk and quirt. On reverse side are two horses and man with quirt. Wood lash pin with brass upholstery tacks driven into each end. Lash native tanned buffalo leather. Chandler-Pohrt Collection 2988.* **11.** *Osage (?), c.1860. Handle 38 cm. lash 59 cm. Engraving suggests military exploits of quirt owner. Figures are men, man on horseback, and horse tracks. On reverse side are engraved curvilinear designs used by Prairie tribes. Holes on each side may indicate use of brass tacks for decoration. Wood lash pin. Lash native tanned leather. Chandler-Pohrt Collection 2989.*

12a,12b. *Crow, c.1875. Handle 45.5 cm, lash 58 cm. Engraved with animals important to Plains Indian economy: buffalo, moose, elk, deer, antelope, bear, crane, a horse; also coniferous trees. Probably engraved by two men: both fine line work and three cruder elk. Reddish brown and black pigments rubbed into the lines. Wood lash pin. Braided lash appears to be later replacement, commercially made, part of drover's whip (?). Partially beaded, painted wrist strap typical Crow work. Chandler-Pohrt Collection 2403.*

13a, 13b. *Crow, c.1875. Handle 46.2 cm, lash 55.5 cm. Unusually long and heavy.* **a:** *deeply engraved lines, cross-hatching; four elk, moose, bear. Upper handle crosshatched in hourglass shape; one elk.* **b:** *large elk and buffalo. Reddish brown and black pigments rubbed into the lines. Lash pin iron nail. Braided lash native tanned leather. Beaded wrist strap classic Crow beadwork. Collected in Montana c.1890 by Charles Henry Palmer. Virginia Ward Golding Collection.*

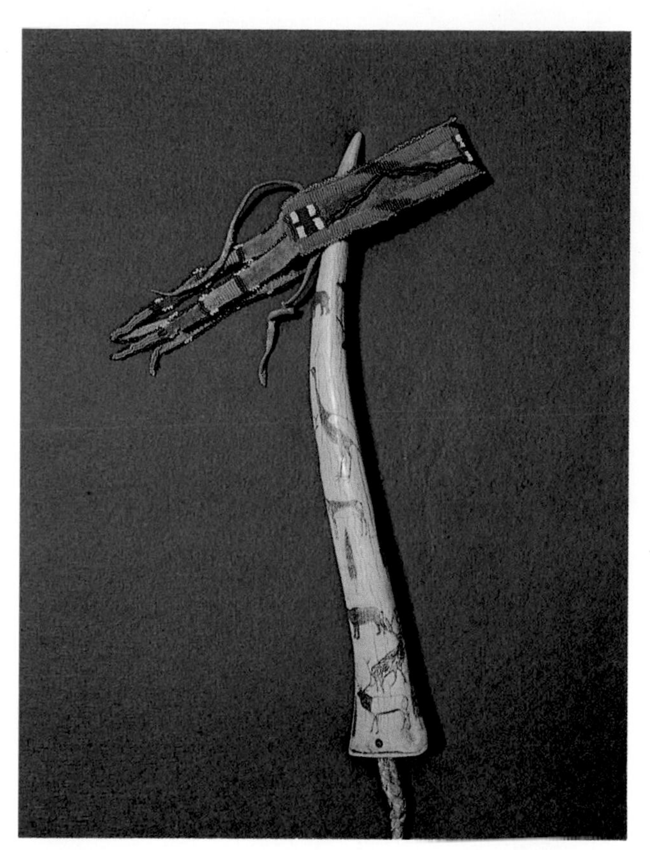

12a

12b

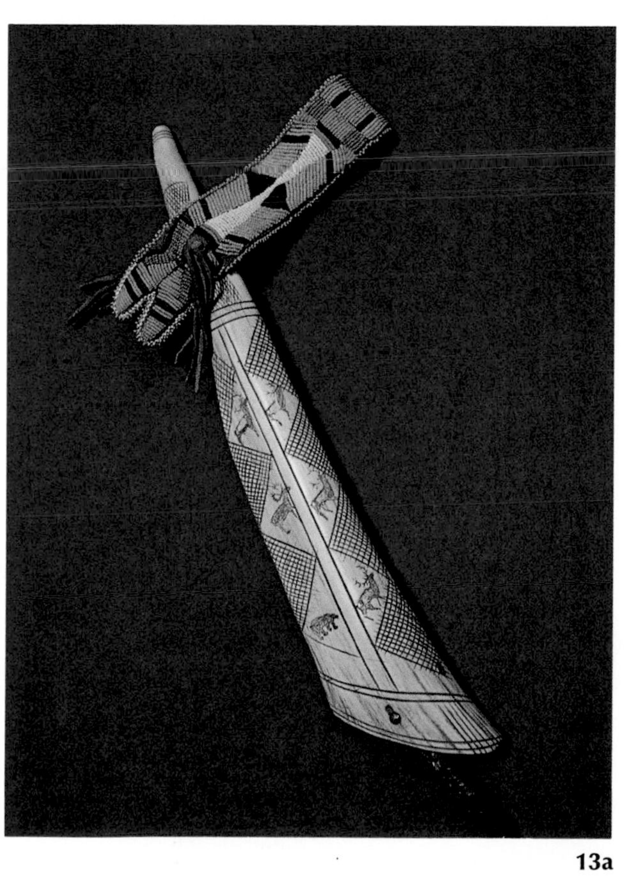

13a

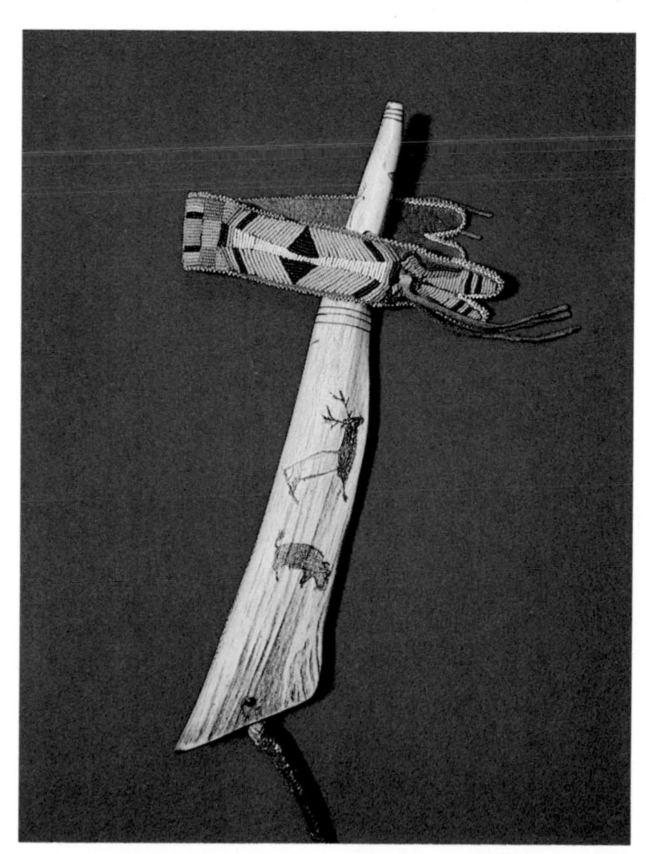

13b

1

THE DYER COLLECTION
AT THE KANSAS CITY MUSEUM

Susan Brown McGreevy

Hence the foundation was laid to what was to become an historically valuable collection . . . for I had secured from nearly every tribe in the United States and Alaska something . . . I veritably became a curio fiend . . . travelling further, going oftener, probing deeper, seeing more, spending more, and getting more than any other seeker in the same direction (Dyer 1896:87).

These words from Ida Casey Dyer's book, *Fort Reno,* refer to what is now the nucleus of the Native American collection at the Kansas City Museum. Of the approximately sixteen hundred artifacts in the collection, eight hundred were acquired by Ida Dyer, and her husband, Colonel Daniel Burns Dyer.

Colonel Dyer was born in Joliet, Illinois, in 1849. At thirteen he joined his father and brother to fight with the Union Army. When he was twenty, Dyer went to work in Baxter Springs (now Kansas) where in 1880 he was appointed to the Quapaw Indian Agency. In August 1884, he became agent to the Cheyenne and Arapaho at Fort Reno (now El Reno, Oklahoma). Although records indicate that Dyer's service at the Quapaw Agency passed without incident, his subsequent appointment with the Cheyenne and Arapaho was less than meritorious. His demonstrable insensitivity toward the Indians, compounded by alleged collusion with Anglo* cattle interests, led to his official suspension in July 1885 (Record Group 48). The end of his employment as Indian agent, however, marked the beginning of a long and profitable business career in Augusta, Georgia, and Kansas City, Missouri.

While the Colonel was occupied with agency business, his wife was preoccupied with acquiring American Indian material. *Fort Reno* not only documents the acquisition of some important pieces in the collection, but also provides a lively account of Mrs. Dyer's experiences during the year she lived at the Cheyenne and Arapaho Agency. Her personal sentiments and biases often reflect that curious combination of romanticism and ethnocentrism so characteristic of nineteenth century Anglo attitudes toward the Indians.

In 1897 the Dyers were divorced, and Mrs. Dyer's holdings reverted to the Colonel as part of the settlement. Dyer continued to collect until his death in 1912. The original D. B. Dyer Collection was shown at several important exhibitions: the National Agricultural Exhibition, Kansas City, Missouri, 1887; the World's Columbian Exposition, Chicago, 1893 (diploma and medal awarded); World's Fair, Omaha, 1898; World's Fair, St. Louis, 1904. For many years the collection was housed in the Kansas City Public Library where it attracted additional donations of Indian material. On July 5, 1940,

*The term Anglo is used here to refer to non-Indians.

1. *War shirt, Cheyenne. Collected 1885. 78 cm high, 63 cm wide. Indian tanned buckskin, organic paints, glass beads, red stroud cloth, scalp locks. Attributed to Stone Calf. Dyer 632, KC 40.623. Photograph by Orville Crane.*

the Daniel B. Dyer Museum trusteeship was transferred from the Kansas City Public School District to the Kansas City Museum Association. The collection has been increased by further acquisitions since 1940.

The Southern Cheyenne and their allies the Arapaho had been reluctant "reservation Indians" for fourteen years when Colonel Dyer assumed his position as their agent. The U.S. government assiduously reinforced the commonly held belief that the solution to the so-called "Indian problem" was to civilize the "savages." According to Ida Dyer, "orders were to compel these people to work, the only road to civilization" (Dyer 1896:55). Therefore the term "Indian agent," which overtly meant paternalistic supervisor, covertly implied catalyst of assimilation. Although the Plains Indians had been physically removed to reservations, their spiritual homeland remained endurably Indian, and the prophesied assimilation never fully materialized.

The collection at the Kansas City Museum is more than a random sampling of "finery worn by 'real live' Indians," of "solid beadwork elaborately ornamented," of "harmonious blendings of color made of dyes of vegetable substances," of "barbaric gems . . . the evidences of soon to be vanished greatness" (Dyer 1896); it is a material reflection of a radically different way of organizing the universe. The "curios" and "gewgaws" that were collected by the Dyers were, in fact, products of people for whom creativity was an integral part of everyday life, and for whom the intimate and reciprocal relationship between man, nature, and the spirit world was a sacred trust.

The fusion of sacred and secular was a pervasive characteristic of Plains creativity, and much of the art embodied a profound mystical symbolism. Colors had ritual associations with the four cardinal directions; quillwork societies received their power from supernatural origins; geometric designs were based on sacred images; naturalistic paintings often derived from supernatural visions. Many pieces in the Dyers' collection reflect these sacred qualities. The shield cover (on the cover of this issue of *American Indian Art Magazine)* is painted with sacred colors and designs. Ideogrammatic power symbols include eagle feathers, painted bear paws, and "life" stripes. A shield was among the most sacrosanct of male possessions, and was always made under holy sanctions (Powell 1977). War shirts also were imbued with sacred significance, and only the most courageous men were allowed to wear them. As representations of past and future victories, such shirts metaphorically symbolized the survival of the tribe. The shirt in Fig. 1 is attributed to Stone Calf, an honored Cheyenne war leader. As an interesting historical footnote, Stone Calf's steadfast defense of his people and traditions was interpreted by Dyer as a direct and personal threat to the agent's authority (Berthrong 1976). Dyer's notes refer to Stone Calf as the "most ruthless, uncompromising, . . . cold blooded scoundrel" (Dyer n.d:17).

Anglo missionary repressions of native religions contributed to the anomie of reservation life, and by 1890 sacred art was on the decline. Artistic creativity gradually became redefined in terms of a more individualized, purely decorative idiom. The use of trade materials, such as stroud cloth and glass beads, stimulated innovations in technique and elaborations of design. Glass beads were not only easier to work with than porcupine quills, they also provided an infinitely broader palette. There are many outstanding pieces of beadwork in the Museum's collection. A cradle (Fig. 2), fully decorated with glass "seed" beads, is a fine example of the textural dimension (reminiscent of quillwork) that can be achieved with lazy-stitch technique. The scroll-like design of the brass-studded wooden headboard is a delicate and unusual piece of Plains wood carving. Mrs. Dyer reports that the cradle was made and used by the daughter of the prominent Sioux chief, Young Man Afraid Of His Horses (Dyer 1896:89). The provenience of

Text continues on page 72

2. *Cradle, Western Sioux. Collected 1885. 105 cm long, 30 cm wide. Glass beads, rawhide, canvas, brass studs, wood. Attributed to daughter of Young Man Afraid Of His Horses. Dyer 611, KC 40.399.* **3.** *Toy horse and rider, Blackfoot. Collected 1885. 23 cm high, 20 cm long. Wooden frame, Indian tanned buckskin, rawhide, glass beads, red stroud cloth, cotton, horsehair. Dyer 5, KC 40.475.* **4.** *Child's belt, Cheyenne. Collected 1885. 56.3 cm long, 30 cm wide. Indian tanned leather, silver conchas, glass beads, tin tinklers, cowrie shells, brass beads, bone hair-pipe beads, rabbit's foot, wooden bead, watch cog, skeleton key. Dyer 41, KC 40.617. Photograph by Jerry Eisterhold.* **5.** *Boy's outfit (shirt, leggings, moccasins), Kiowa?/Osage. (Cheyenne moccasins.) c.1900. 73 cm long (overall), 46 cm wide (overall). Indian tanned buckskin, organic paint. KC L27.40.140.* **6.** *Woman's boots, Kiowa or Comanche. c.1880. 52 cm high, 23 cm long (at foot). Indian tanned buckskin, rawhide, organic paints, glass beads, brass studs. KC 39.41.463. All photographs except* **4** *by Orville Crane.*

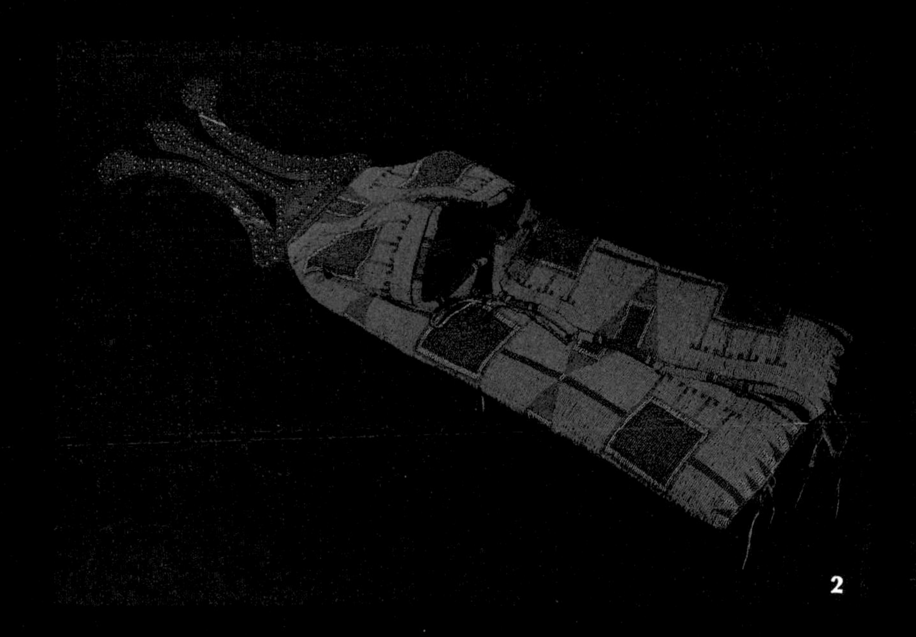
2

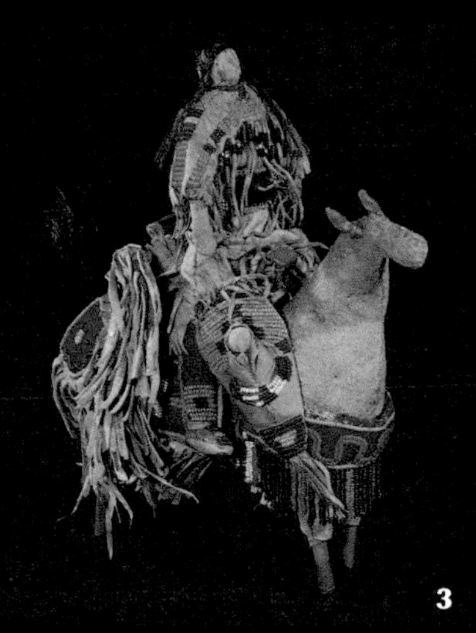
3

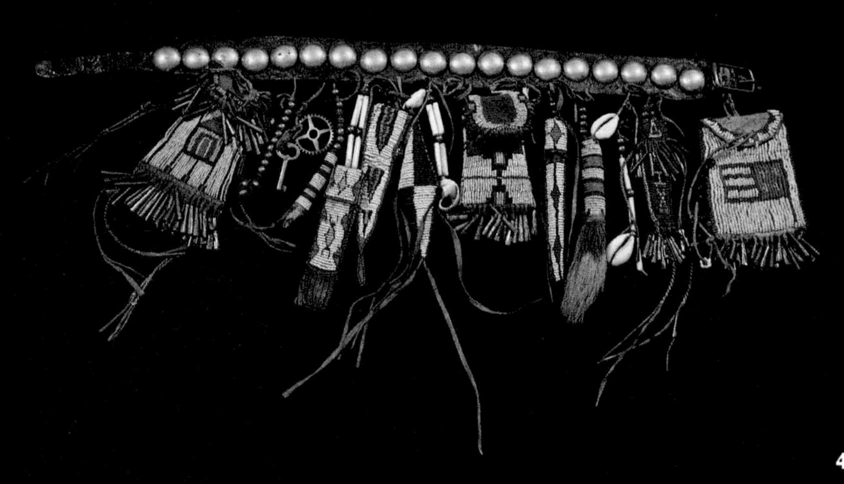
4

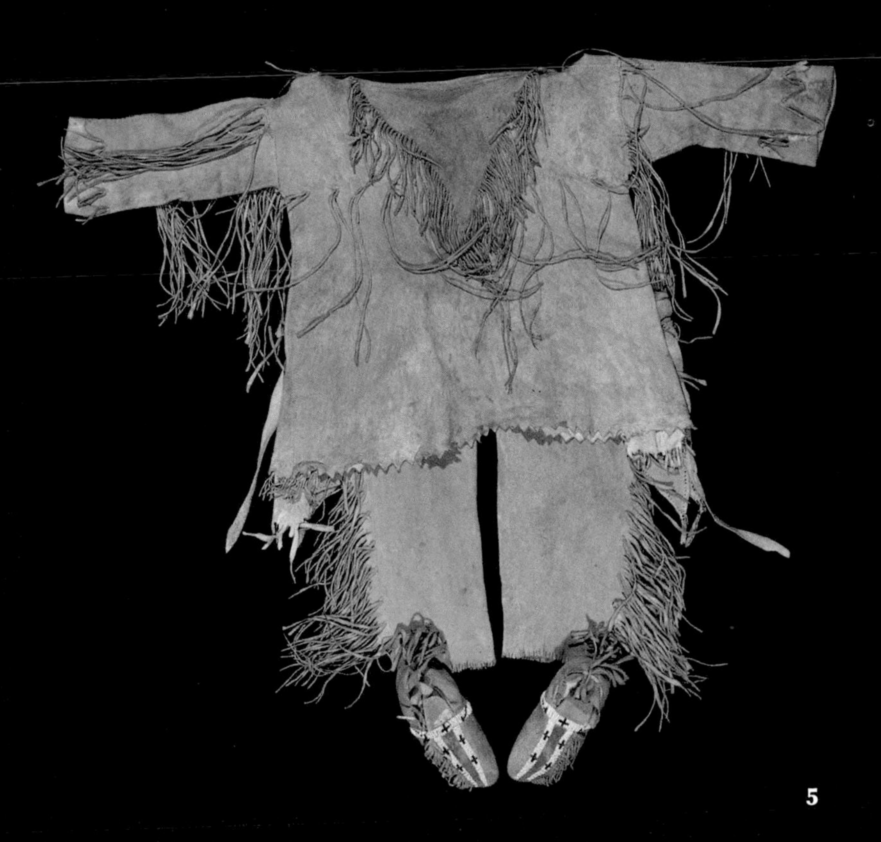
5

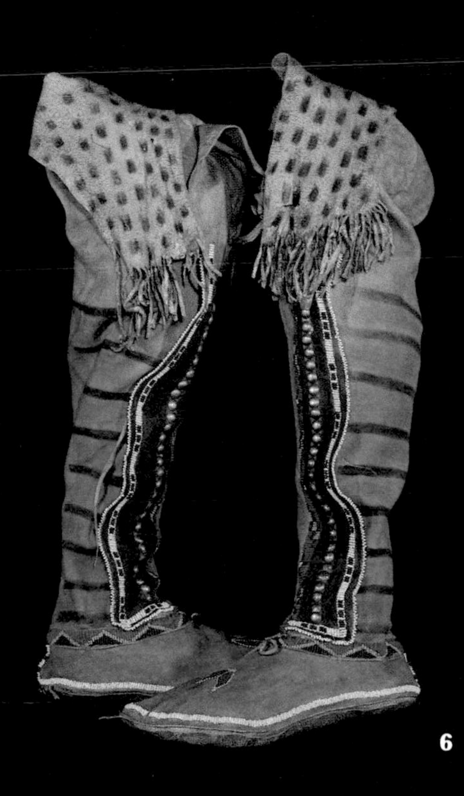
6

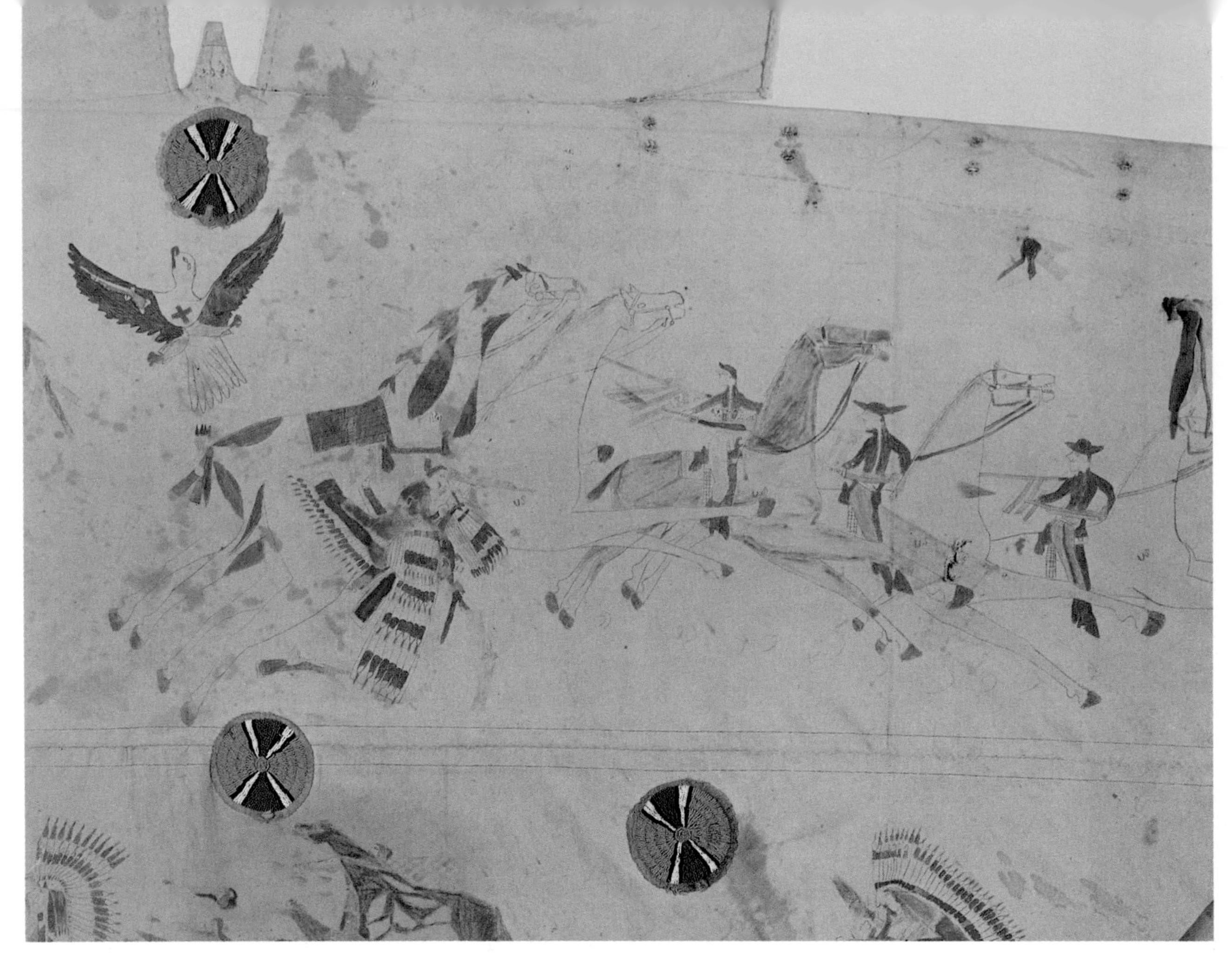

7

7. *Tipi canvas (detail), Ute/Cheyenne. Collected 1885. 126 cm long, 102 cm high. Canvas, indelible inks, organic paints, colored pencils, glass beads. Painted by Yellow Nose. Dyer 704, KC 40.229.*
8. *Basketry hat, Nootka. c.1800. 17 cm high, 35.5 cm diameter. Spruce root, organic paints. Dyer 496. Photographs by Orville Crane.*

8

the cradle was the subject of some controversy when it appeared in the "Sacred Circles" exhibition. Because many people argued that it had a distinctly Cheyenne look, it was so labeled (Coe 1977:177) although the Sioux attribution is clearly documented in *Fort Reno*.

Some artifacts in the collection reflect the individualized personal approach. The horse and rider in Fig. 3 not only represent hours of loving maternal creativity, they also provide detail in miniature of cradleboard, clothing, and horse trappings. The woman who made the Kiowa boots (Fig. 6) had a fine eye for the aesthetics of contrast.

The child's belt in Fig. 4 illustrates the inventive quality of Plains art. The story of its purchase provides a colorful description of Mrs. Dyer's collecting mania:

> I heard a jingling, rattling, and a running of pattering feet one day . . . and found a number of tidy-looking Cheyenne women of the 'smartest' of their set, with their children, standing looking in my window . . . One of the party was a little nabob of a girl . . . royally dressed . . . At first, I negotiated with the mother for her just as she stood before me . . . I was fully satisfied however, when I succeeded in inducing, by a most liberal offer, to have her part with the heirloom belt she wore (Dyer 1896:95).

Another example of cultural interaction is the child's outfit in Fig. 5. It is part of the Schmelzer collection on permanent loan to the Museum since 1940. Although it was collected Osage, the style of the shirt and leggings is Kiowa. The Osage took advantage of the proximity of the many tribes that were removed to Indian Territory, and frequently commissioned them to make articles of clothing and ornamentation for Osage use.

Men often painted realistic depictions of valorous deeds and notable battles on clothing, robes and tipis. The painted canvas tipi (Fig. 7) portrays the Cheyenne fighting with the U.S. Army during the Battle of Washita in 1868. Note the U.S. brand on the army horses and the war-adorned tails of the Cheyenne horses. The protagonist of the painting is Black Kettle, an eminent Cheyenne council chief. In his concern for the survival of his people, Black Kettle consistently tried to maintain peaceful relations with Anglo intruders into his territory. It is therefore singularly ironic that Black Kettle's band was the victim of the most flagrant U.S. Army attacks. By 1885 the infamous Battle of Washita had become part of Cheyenne oral tradition. Mrs. Dyer commissioned the painting, and the artist was an adopted Cheyenne. *Fort Reno* provides collection details:

> The hand painted tepee that 'Yellow-Nose' . . . has so artistically portrayed for me is of that same battle [Washita] . . . 'Yellow-Nose' was captured from a fighting band of Utes when a boy by the Cheyennes . . . He grew up with the tribe . . . My tepee canvas was drawn [with] a number of sticks . . . that he used for brushes. A bottle of indelible black ink, red ink, and colored pencils . . . all kinds of dyes and colored powders made from Indian herbs comprised his materials (Dyer 1896:96).

The largest part of the collection consists of southern and central Plains material because of the Dyers' contribution, and Kansas City's geographic proximity to the Great Plains. However, the collection is not exclusively Plains. There are representative artifacts from the Eastern Woodlands, the Southwest, the Northwest Coast, and the Far North. Thus the collection reflects the diversity of North American Indian art. One of the finest non-Plains specimens is included here for illustration. Twined and painted basketry hats are fairly common among Northwest Coast tribes; however, the black-painted Nootka version (Fig. 8) is a superb example of a relatively rare form. Bill Holm, curator of Northwest Coast Indian art at the Burke Memorial Museum, Seattle, has located only about twenty of these hats.

Ida Dyer was wrong. Indian greatness has not vanished. Cultures are dynamic: they can and do change, they can and do survive. Indian art is not static and frozen in time — or in museums either, for that matter. Its persistence reflects the viability of a unique traditional heritage: its changes reflect the creative vitality of the human experience.

Bibliography

Berthong, Donald J.
1976 *The Cheyenne and Arapaho ordeal.* University of Oklahoma Press, Norman, Okla.

Coe, Ralph T.
1977 *Sacred Circles: two thousand years of North American Indian art.* Nelson Gallery Foundation, Kansas City, Mo.

Dyer, Daniel Burns and Edward Butts
n.d. Catalogue of Col D. B. Dyer's Collection at the Public Library Museum, Kansas City, Mo. Unpublished manuscript.

Dyer, Mrs. D. B.
1896 *Fort Reno, or picturesque Cheyenne and Arapaho Army life before the opening of Oklahoma.* G. W. Dillingham Publishers, New York.

Holm, Bill
1977 Personal communications

Marriott, Alice
1956 The trade guilds of Southern Cheyenne women. *Bulletin of the Oklahoma Anthropological Society,* Vol. IV.

Moore, John H.
1974 A study of religious symbolism among Cheyenne Indians. Unpublished Ph.D. dissertation. Department of Anthropology, New York University.

Pohrt, Richard A.
1975 Observations on the flag motif in Indian art. *The American Indian: The American Flag.* Flint Institute of Arts, Flint, Mich.

Powell, Father Peter J.
1977 Beauty for new life. *Native American Heritage.* Chicago Art Institute, Chicago.

Record Group 48
1885 Records of the Office of the Secretary of the Interior, Appointments Division, Charges File. National Archives, Washington, D.C.

Susan Brown McGreevy was curator of North American ethnology at the Kansas City Museum (1975-1977) where her research concentrated on southern and central Plains tribes, especially the Osage and the Cheyenne. She is currently curator and acting director of The Wheelwright Museum in Santa Fe.

Pipes continued from page 55

Bibliography

Catlin, George
1841 *Letters and notes on the manners, customs, and condition of the North American Indians.* 2 vols. Egyptian Hall, Piccadilly, London.

Ewers, John C.
1967 William Clark's Indian Museum in St. Louis, 1816-1838. In *A Cabinet of Curiosities. Five Episodes in the Evolution of American Museums,* edited by Walter Muir Whitehill. The University of Virginia Press, Charlottesville, Va.
1978 *Indian art in pipestone. George Catlin's illustrated portfolio in the British Museum,* edited by John C. Ewers. The Smithsonian Institution Press, Washington, D.C.

Feest, Christian
1968 *Indianer Nordamerikas.* Museum für Völkerkunde, Vienna.

Nicollet, Joseph N.
1872 Memoir of J. N. Nicollet. *Minnesota Historical Society Collections,* Vol. I. St. Paul, Minn.

Schoolcraft, Henry Rowe
1854 *Historical and statistical information respecting the history, condition and prospects of the Indian tribes of the United States,* Part II. Lippencott, Grambo, Philadelphia.

John C. Ewers, senior ethnologist at the Smithsonian Institution, has studied Plains Indian history and art in the field, in libraries and in museums of this country and abroad for more than forty years. His Murals in the Round: Painted Tipis of the Kiowa and Kiowa-Apache Indians *will be published this fall. Current projects include compiling a history of collecting among the Plains Indians, a revision of his first book,* Plains Indian Painting *(1939), and completion of a pioneer book on* Plains Indian Sculpture.

Caesar continued from page 61

1976 *Contemporary Southern Plains Indian metalwork,* catalogue for an exhibition organized by the Indian Arts and Crafts Board of the United States Department of the Interior, Anadarko, Oklahoma, in cooperation with the Oklahoma Indian Arts and Crafts Cooperative.

Feder, Norman

1962 Plains Indian metalworking with emphasis on hair plates. *American Indian Tradition,* Vol. VIII, No. 2, pp. 55-76, Alton, Illinois.

1962 Plains Indian metalworking part two. *American Indian Tradition,* Vol. VIII, No. 3, pp. 93-110, Alton, Illinois.

La Barre, Weston

1970 *The Peyote Cult.* The Shoe String Press, Inc., Hamden, Conn.

Rosemary Ellison is the supervisor of museums, exhibitions, and publications of the Indian Arts and Crafts Board of the United States Department of the Interior.

Persons interested in acquiring German silver metalwork should contact Julius and Harry Caesar at Caesar's Indian Metalcrafts, P.O. Box 435, Pawnee, Oklahoma 74058. Bruce Caesar is accepting a limited number of special commissions and inquiries should be sent directly to him at P.O. Box 1183, Anadarko, Oklahoma 73005. Another source of German silver metalwork by the Caesars and other outstanding Southern Plains Indian metalsmiths is the Oklahoma Indian Arts and Crafts Cooperative, an Indian owned and operated arts and crafts enterprise which operates the sales shop located in the Southern Plains Indian Museum in Anadarko, Oklahoma. For those interested in learning more about contemporary Native American metalwork in German silver, an exhibition catalogue, Contemporary Southern Plains Indian Metalwork, *is available from the Oklahoma Indian Arts and Crafts Cooperative, Box 966, Anadarko, Oklahoma 73005, $5.50 including postage.*

Museums continued from page 30

Southern Plains Indian Museum and Crafts Center
Anadarko, Oklahoma
"Contemporary Southern Plains Indian Arts and Crafts" (through September 30); custom-made knives by Ted Miller, Peoria-Miami (Oct. 15-Nov. 23). The annual American Indian Exposition (August 14-19) will be held adjacent to the Museum.

University of British Columbia
Vancouver, British Columbia
An exhibition of Washo basketry will be presented in the Fine Arts Gallery during the International Congress of Americanists (August 10-17).

The Wheelwright Museum
Santa Fe, New Mexico
"American Indian Art Now" (through September 3), an invitational show selected by J. J. Brody, director of the Maxwell Museum of Anthropology, and Neil Parsons, Blackfoot artist, has been dedicated to the memory of T. C. Cannon. "Hopi Art Now" (Oct. 6-Nov. 14) will include paintings by the Artist Hopid, jewelry by Charles Loloma, and contemporary basketry, pottery and kachinas. All works on display will be for sale. Patricia Janis Broder, author of *Hopi Painting: The World of the Hopis,* will be present October 6 to autograph copies of her new book.

Art from museums in the Southwest has been loaned to Vice President and Mrs. Walter F. Mondale; it will hang in their official residence through April 1979. Among the Indian artists whose work is exhibited are R. C. Gorman, Michael Naranjo, Joy Navasie, Garnet Pavatea, Fritz Scholder, Daisy Taugelchee, Laura Tomasie, and Elizabeth White.

DECISION ON FEATHERED ARTIFACTS

On June 7, 1978, the United States District Court, District of Colorado, found for the plaintiffs — owners of, dealers in, and appraisers of American Indian art — and against the Secretary of the Interior and the officials of the United States Fish and Wildlife Service in an important legal case involving the possession and sale of feathered artifacts. The court decided that the rights of the plaintiffs to sell or trade their feathered artifacts which predated the federal law could not be prohibited. Depending upon the type of feathers, the dates of federal protection range from 1918 to 1974.

The case was built strongly on constitutionally guaranteed property rights; it claimed that abrogation of those rights without due process of law was prohibited by the Fifth Amendment. Furthermore, the plaintiffs pointed out that prohibiting the sale of old feathered artifacts does not achieve the apparent objectives of the Fish and Wildlife Service in the protection of living birds.

On July 5, the defendants appealed the District Court's decision to the Supreme Court of the United States.

FEATHERS

Sara J. Wolf

The universality of feathers in ethnographic collections presents a preservation challenge to conservators and collectors. Feather conservation methods have not been widely published, nor has a great deal of research been done on the subject; consequently, there are few answers to the questions of dealing with the restoration or conservation of feather materials. For this reason, the greatest emphasis should be on keeping collections from deteriorating.

The feathers generally found in greatest numbers in ethnographic collections are the flight feathers of the adult bird. These feathers are composed of the shaft — the central axis — which supports the vane. The shaft ends in the quill which was originally embedded in the skin of the bird. The vane, or barbs, are actually outgrowths of the shaft which interlock with one another by means of small hooks to form the cohesive structure of the feather. Any damage to the hooks on the ends of the barbs causes the barbs to separate and the feather to lose its characteristic shape.

In addition to the adult feather, softer down feathers are sometimes found in collections. These are the first coat of the young bird, and so lack the cohesive structure of the adult feather. The down should not be confused with the soft, unarticulated basal fluff sometimes found at the base of adult feathers, but the treatment and care of both are similar, and because of the less rigid structure, present different problems from those of adult feathers.

Feathers are protein material and so are susceptible to degradation by microorganisms (mold and fungi), moths and other pests. Moths and some insects actually digest some components of the protein material and can leave the collector with a few fragments instead of an object. Mold and fungi generally prosper in environments of high relative humidity and warmth and can cause permanent damage and staining of the object as they secrete protein digesting enzymes. This suggests the need for fumigants and fungicides in the event of an infestation, and even more importantly, the need for careful display and storage techniques which guard against these pests. However, not all of the fumigants and fungicides available may be safe for feather collections and a conservator should be consulted before a collection is so treated.

Protein is subject to denaturation by excess moisture and dessication by excessive heat and dryness. The natural oil of the feather, which acted as a lubricant and sometimes as a water repellent for the bird, aids in trapping dust and dirt in the barbs, which in turn attracts insects and other pests. It has already been pointed out that breaking the hooks on the ends of the barbs will cause the feather to lose its shape. This also leaves the feather open to a greater chance of damage by abrasion, the loss of the barbs themselves, and damage to the shaft. In addition, the shaft, which tends

Text continues on page 78

NOTE: As editor of the series on conservation of American Indian artifacts, I am attempting to present information which will be of general interest to collectors and museum personnel on the care of anthropological collections. Though the series cannot give specific conservation treatments, I hope that it will create a general awareness of the needs of collections and give enough information so that problems can be recognized in time to refer them to professionals. *S.J.W.*

to become brittle with age and loss of natural moisture, can bend or break under even slight pressure.

Dust and dirt are the primary problems for feather collections. Polyethylene bags are very useful for storage, but it is important to make sure that the feathered object is free of dirt and evidence of biological infestation, since the bag will create a microenvironment of its own.

Feathers are almost always found in conjunction with other materials, such as wood, leather and fiber, and may have been glued or tied onto a support. They may have been dyed or split along the shaft and curled. Because of the variety of conditions in which a feather may be found, any cleaning or conservation treatment must be tailored to the particular instance. The cleaning method chosen will also depend on the physical condition of the feather; whether or not it is whole; whether or not it has been broken.

The choices presented to the conservator for cleaning feathers fall into the following categories: mechanical, solvent, dry cleaning, and combinations of the three. If feathers are attached to an object which cannot be treated by solvent cleaning, mechanical cleaning methods are the only choice. This would involve such methods as brushing with a soft brush or cotton swab. Brushing presents the possibility of damage to the hooks on the barbs, and must be carried out with extreme care. In addition, cotton fibers from the swab may catch in the feather, particularly in the basal fluff or down feathers, causing the barbs to pull apart, or to be torn away from the shaft. Other mechanical methods available are dusting with compressed air in a gentle stream, or vacuuming under low suction power if the feather has been placed between wire mesh screens to prevent damage or loss to the barbs.

These fairly gentle cleaning methods are relatively without controversy because they do not physically or chemically modify the feather. They may not, however, produce a sufficiently clean object because the dirt may be trapped by the oil inherent in the feather. Solvent cleaning has been recommended in the past, but the potential for damage is considerable.

Wetting the feather with water, or with water and a mild detergent may loosen dirt; also warm water has been recommended to encourage straightening of bent feather shafts.

However, serious consideration should be given to the consequences of wetting protein material because of its susceptibility of hydrolysis. Any cleaning with detergent would require successive rinsings, and prolonged contact with water would only serve to encourage weakening and deterioration of the feathers. In addition, wet cleaning tends to loosen the grip of the barb hooks, allowing the barbs to become matted and separated. It also tends to tangle the basal fluff, and once the cohesive structure of the feather is disturbed, it is a very difficult and time-consuming operation to realign each barb (Fig. 1).

Dry cleaning solvents and spirit soaps have also been suggested as cleaning agents. The problem here is that dry solvent cleaning removes not only the dirt, but the natural oils in the feather. Although the oil is the primary attraction for dirt, it also keeps the feather flexible, and so should not be removed. Consideration has been given to replacing the oil lost in dry solvent cleaning with a substance such as paraffin oil, or a flexible consolidating material, but these substances could only imitate not duplicate, the function of the natural oil of the feather, and the harsh effects of stripping the oil out of the feather cannot be negated by the application of such materials.

Another dry cleaning method is the use of a dry powder such as talcum, dusted on the feather and then brushed or vacuumed off. Presumably the talc absorbs the excess oil and consequently the dirt. Removal of the powder, however, is not particularly easy and often more powder is left in the crevices between the barbs than is removed.

The choice of a mending or consolidating material for feathers should be determined by the compatibility of the material with the feather, and, more importantly, the reversibility or redispersability of the method and material.

It is possible to mend a feather, but adhesive alone is generally inadequate to hold a broken shaft in place, and so there is a question of what kind of a support to use. Consolidating materials for badly decayed feathers have not been adequately tested and studied for their long-term effects on feathers, so as with mending and cleaning methods, no concrete recommendations can be made, and specific objects should be referred to a conservator for

Text continues on page 80

Irving Toddy "In the Morning" Oil

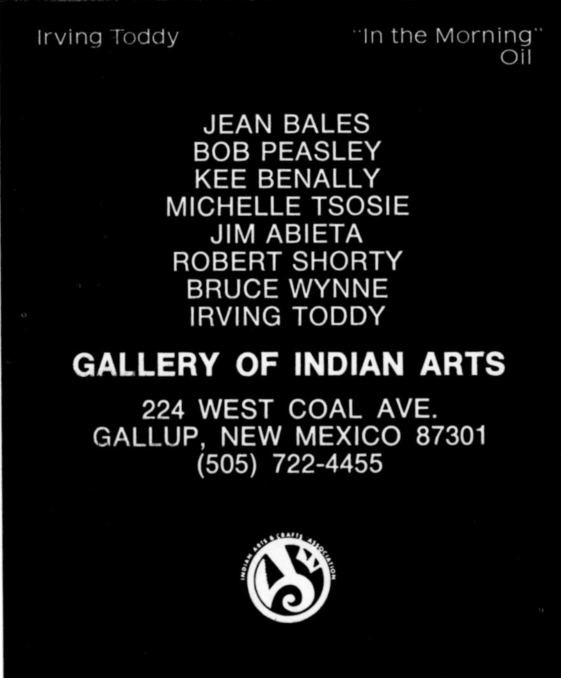

Text continued from page 79

potential treatment. Again, the best possible treatment is proper handling in storage and display situations.

There are some ethical questions to consider in regard to restoration which involves replacing damaged or missing feathers. The extent of conservation and restoration treatments should be based on thorough study of the object, and on documented evidence of the original condition of the object where possible. In some cases, such as strengthening an object which has been structurally weakened by the loss of feathers, or for display purposes, it may be desirable to replace missing feathers. The Northwest Coast mask is missing many of its original feathers (Fig. 2). In this case there was documented evidence that the row of feathers was complete at the time the mask was collected. Complete documentation of the restoration includes photographs with overlays indicating where new feathers were added. No suggestion has been made that any of the additions were part of the original mask, nor were any of the original feathers removed (Fig. 3).

In summary, there is no formula available for the treatment of feather collections except for meticulous attention to those aspects of preventative maintenance which should be practiced for the preservation of any collection. The feather, so commonly used and so uncommonly beautiful in its grace and multitude of colors, is an important part of cultural history — important enough to be treated with tremendous respect and care.

Bibliography

Govier, T.
1970 Feathers and featherwork. *Recent Advances in Conservation*. April, 1970.

Gowers, H.J.
1968 Featherwork and its conservation. *Recent Advances in Conservation*. March, 1968.

———
1972 Ethnographical featherwork, edited by J.E. Leene. *Textile Conservation*. Smithsonian Institution Press, Washington, D.C.

Lucas, A.M. and P.R. Stettenheim
1972 *Avian anatomy; integument*. 2 Vols. U.S. Government Printing Office, Washington, D.C.

Voitkevich, A.A.
1966 *The feathers and plumage of birds*. Sidgwick & Jackson, London.

Ms. Wolf is a private anthropological conservator.

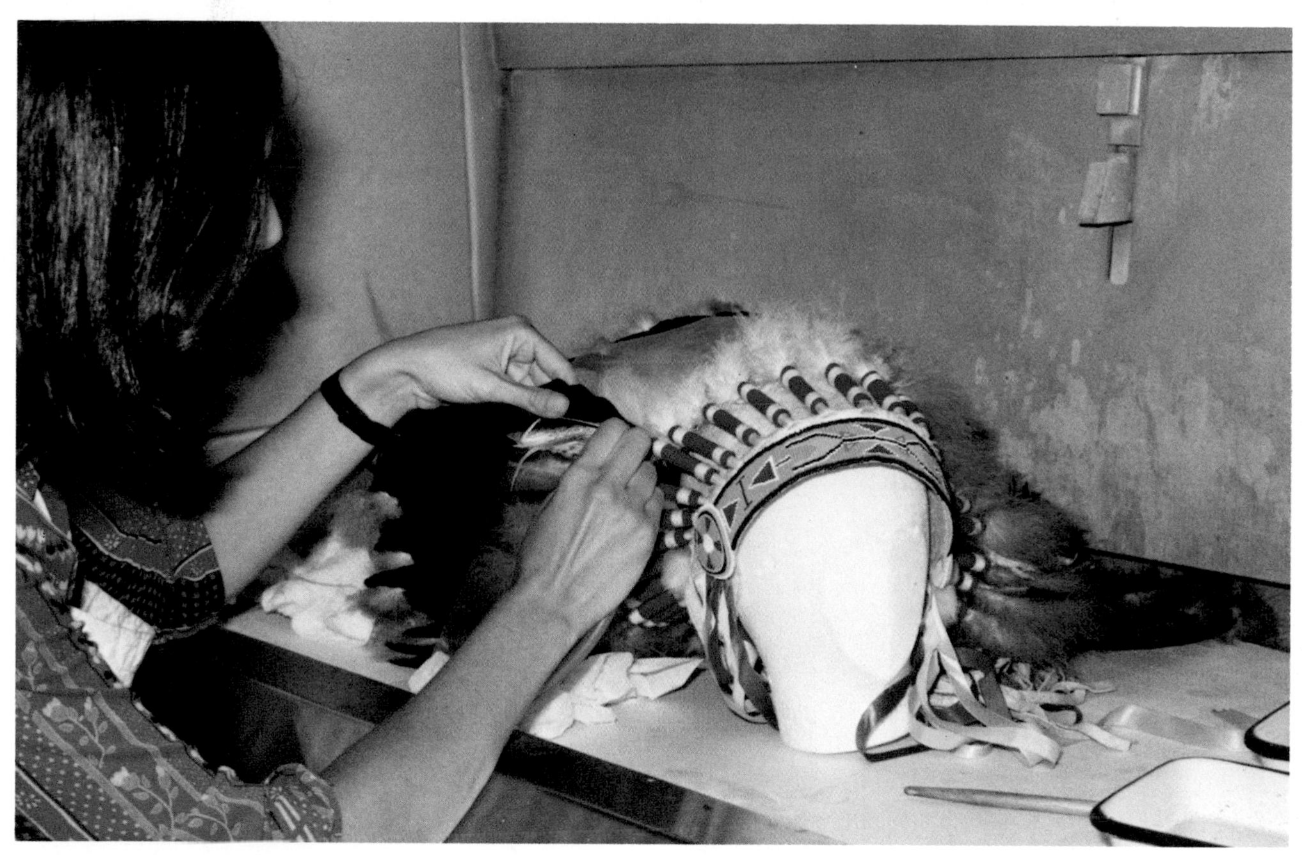

1. *Treatment of an eagle feather headdress by Jane Norman. Each feather has been individually cleaned and the barbs realigned.*

2. *Northwest Coast mask before restoration treatment.*

3. *Northwest Coast mask after treatment. Restoration by Sonja Fogle.*

Photographs courtesy of the Anthropology Conservation Lab, Smithsonian Institution.

To the Navajo all things are alive with the spirit of their creation. The spirit of man shapes his creation. Creation shapes his spirit. Spirit evolves; creation is never complete.

The experiences of life shape each of those who live it. Joy and tragedy, conflict and harmony are woven together and extended in the mind over generations of oral and symbolic tradition.

For many the icons of this tradition have become fixed and stylized. Not so for Boyd Tsosie.

His jewelry interprets his life and the lives of his people with a sense of freedom. He uses the symbols, but in his own fluid style. A style which is constantly changing; reflecting the traditions of his people and the evolving expression of his own feelings and reflections on life.

The materials are precious stones and metals and other things of the earth. The ingredients are earth, sky, plants, animals and all the creations of nature. The theme is – as it has always been for the Navajo – harmony.

Reflecting on harmony leads to an analysis of discord. To appreciate joy is to have known sadness. Tsosie takes his history and that of his people and uses it as a medium of expression, interpreting events and conditions uniquely through his craft.

Each piece has a story, some known only to the artist. Each is an interpretation of the emotions connected with that story.

In his art as in his being – life determines.

Hukahēe Fine Arts Gallery

Specializing in Indian Art

7148 East Stetson Drive • Scottsdale, Arizona 85251 • (602) 994-4503

ADVERTISER INDEX

Contemporary Hopi jewelry by Duane Maktima

nadler's
indian arts

6328 N. Scottsdale Rd
Scottsdale, AZ 85253

602-948-4180